THE
CONQUEST
OF
CANAAN

Jessie Penn-Lewis

THE CONQUEST OF CANAAN

Warfare and Victory
in the Christian Life

CLC PUBLICATIONS
Fort Washington, PA 19034

Published by CLC Publications

U.S.A.
P.O. Box 1449, Fort Washington, PA 19034

GREAT BRITAIN
51 The Dean, Alresford, Hants. SO24 9BJ

AUSTRALIA
P.O. Box 419M, Manunda, QLD 4879

NEW ZEALAND
10 MacArthur Street, Feilding

ISBN 0-87508-943-7

Originally published by
THE OVERCOMER LITERATURE TRUST
England

First American edition
1989
Second American edition
(contemporized)
1992
This printing 2002

Printed in the United States of America

CONTENTS

Prefatory Note

*T*HE addresses on the Book of Joshua given in the following pages were delivered at meetings for Christian workers during the early months of 1911. They were delivered extempore, and with no further preparation than an outline of texts. My purpose was only to give a bird's-eye view of the battlefield of conflict, as depicted in the story of Israel's war in Canaan, and as these four addresses were delivered at intervals of about a month, the matter is not as consecutive in style and condensed in Bible exegesis as it would have been if prepared directly for print. Nevertheless, as the addresses contain light on the warfare with the powers of darkness which may be of service to the Lord's people at this time, I send them forth with all their imperfections upon them, looking to the Spirit of God to give truth to those who need it.

Jessie Penn-Lewis
Leicester
April, 1911

Unless otherwise noted, all scriptures are quoted from the English Revised Version of 1881.

1

How Israel crossed the Jordan—the leader prepared for his work—the sending of the spies—the crossing of Jordan and the buried stones—Jordan the type of Calvary and identification with Christ—the new nation and new life—the knife at Gilgal—the Captain with the drawn sword—the Jericho victory—the defeat at Ai.

LET us take the whole book of Joshua in order to get a bird's-eye view of our spiritual battlefield. To do this we shall need rapidly to refer to chapters rather than verses, so that we may see how wonderfully it pictures the battle in the heavenly places described by the Apostle

Paul in the Epistle to the Ephesians.

This story of Joshua and the people of Israel on the edge of Jordan, and how they crossed to Canaan and entered into warfare to possess the land, is a very remarkable type of the Church of Christ and its passage to the battlefield. In the first chapter of the book you see the human leader, chosen of the Lord to lead Israel over Jordan into Canaan and throughout the campaign there. Joshua is really the Old Testament word for Jesus—Joshua=Jesus—and he is chosen to lead Israel into Canaan. He is commanded to be strong, with his only equipment the Word of God and implicit obedience to it! *Such was Christ's equipment.* The Lord said He *lived* by the Word of God, and that His meat was to do the will of His Father. All that Joshua had to do was to take the directions given to him by God and to lead under His command. Then, God said, "Thou shalt cause this people to inherit the land."

There are hymns depicting Canaan as heaven, but there is no sin in heaven, and no war there. There were both in Israel's Canaan. It is a picture really of a stage in the Christian life. There is the wilderness stage, out of which Joshua leads Israel through Jordan into Canaan, and on the Canaan side is the war to take possession of the land. On the wilderness side of Jordan, the people were occupied with their own troubles as to what they should do.

For instance, they needed water, and when they could not get it they were filled with a murmuring spirit; that was the wilderness stage, where Moses, the man of God, had to bear with them, and stand between them and God—sometimes as intercessor, so that God would not destroy them.

There came a time, however, when God said to Joshua, "Moses My servant is dead; now therefore arise, go over this Jordan, thou, and all this people, unto the land which I give them, even to the children of Israel" (Joshua 1:2); and *"Every place that the sole of your foot shall tread upon, to you have I given it"* (v. 3).

Before they crossed the Jordan, they had a declaration from God that every place that the sole of their feet should tread upon HAD BEEN GIVEN THEM; but they had to walk over it, and take it foot by foot—for God did not hand it over to them and say, "Now you have it," so that they had nothing further to do. He said, "I *have* given it. Now *you* must take it step by step." It was very important that Joshua should be clear on the point that the land in front of him had been given by Jehovah to Israel *before* he started out to *take* it, however, so that always he should act from the faith position of assured victory.

This promise of the land already given is followed by a second promise made directly to Joshua in verse 5, *"There shall not any man be able to stand before thee all the days of thy life. . . . I will not fail thee nor forsake thee."*

But as we read on, we see how on Joshua's part it was necessary he should be strong and courageous, so as to cooperate with God for the fulfillment of these promises. How the words ring out in power: *"Only be thou strong and very courageous, and then shalt thou cause this people to inherit the land."* These words make it appear that Joshua was responsible for the courage. "ONLY be thou strong . . . ," said Jehovah. This is what every child of God must take heed to in the battle of today. We are responsible not to get depressed or discouraged for a moment by yielding to the temptations of the enemy to look away from God. You must settle it that all discouragement is from the enemy, and not under any circumstances yield to or accept it.

Then again, Joshua is not left in any doubt as to how he is to become full of courage. He is bidden to turn to the commandments of God as written in the Law: *"Observe to do according to all the Law. . . . Turn not from it to the right hand nor to the left, that thou mayest have good success."* Implicit, undeviating obedience to the Word of God. *"This Book of the Law shall not depart out of thy mouth, but thou shalt meditate thereon day and night"* (v. 8). If Joshua had lived today, how much time would he give to the reading of "novels"? Yes, we may well ask if he would have been a valiant leader to Israel in leading them to victory if he had fed upon much of the literature of the present time.

It is useless expecting success or victory in this spiritual battlefield unless we are prepared to take the Word of God as our one authority. We must be prepared for implicit, undeviating obedience to the Word of God. There must not be a turning from the Word in the slightest measure, to the right or to the left. We must make sure of what God's Book says, and then stand to it without questioning, and God will be with us. It is the one great condition of success—this implicit recognition of the authority of God's Word and obedience to it, honestly seeking to know the will of God. And not merely implicit obedience to one text, but seeking to know and to do God's will as revealed in the general principles laid down in His Word for life and conduct.

The only way to be strong and very courageous is to be filled with the Word of God, and to have the mind full of it by meditating upon it. Not simply reading a little and then putting the Book down, but really meditating on God's Word until you know the heart-truth of all that is written in the sacred Book.

"Meditate thereon day and night, that thou mayest observe to do [it] . . . for then shalt thou make thy way prosperous, and then thou shalt have good success. Have I not commanded thee? Be strong and of good courage;

be not affrighted, neither be thou dismayed: for the LORD thy God is with thee" (Joshua 1:8–9).

In this passage, we also see from the Lord's words the linking together of His Presence and the resulting courage and fearlessness necessary for victory. To be freed from all fear and dismay of the forces of the enemy, our great remedy is to have God's Word strengthening us day and night, so that we lose sight of man and all fear of man. This Word is strength to you. You would be strong Christians if you were so filled with the Word of God that everything you heard around you would instantly cause to spring into your mind the passage which would meet or explain the need— so that whatever question was asked you, or whatever doubt came to you, in one moment there would come the right answer to your mind from the Scriptures.

Are you being kept by God at this point? You know so much about victory, you know so much about identification with Christ and His cross; but are you *strong and very courageous?* Are you dismayed, are you afraid, are you fearful? Will you allow all fear to be swept from you and go forward meditating on this Book day and night? It means when you awake in the morning the revelation that is fresh will be in your mind. When you go to sleep, it means that you will not have troublesome thoughts in your mind to prevent you from sleeping. One great, strong, mighty resource for unbroken victory is to be filled with divine strength by this Word dwelling in you richly. This was the provision for Joshua as he was starting out, and if you are to be a "leader"—to be able to lead souls around you into Canaan, or to the heavenly places—you can only have the true vision to lead them when the Word dwells in you and you meditate upon it, as Joshua was bidden to do.

Remember, too, they were not all "Joshuas"! Joshua had his place and commission, and the people had theirs. If you try to be a "Joshua" when the Lord wants you to be one of the people, it will only mean confusion and disorder. True, God can make you a "Joshua" in your own center and sphere, to lead those around you into the heavenly places; but it is necessary to ask you if you are ready to recognize others with a commission from God which was not granted to you? And are you willing to cooperate with others called of God, and not simply act on your own in relation to other members of the Body of Christ?

In this campaign Joshua sent out spies to spy out the land, and, according to the second chapter, when the spies returned, they reported that the terror of God was already upon the people of Canaan. That was a great thing gained. It strengthened Joshua. He found that what the Lord had told him was already working. It is really true when you go forward in aggressive warfare in this spiritual battlefield *that you will find the fear of God already upon the enemy*. If we understood it, the powers of darkness must tremble when they see the children of God appropriating the victory of Christ and starting forward in aggressive warfare. If the whole Church would rise up in the strength and the might of God, the principalities and the powers would be beaten down, for the *fear of God is already upon them*.

In chapter 3, Joshua issued the call to the people to get ready to cross the Jordan, and chapter 4 tells of the actual crossing. The priests were sent first, and they carried with them the ark of the Lord. They took their stand in the center of Jordan, and stood there until all the people had passed over it. The priests were told to take from the center of Jordan twelve stones, and they were to bury in Jordan also twelve stones. The stones thus buried represented the twelve tribes of Israel left buried in Jordan's waters; and the twelve stones taken out of Jordan and carried into Canaan represented the new nation, stepping out of the waters which were actually waters of death to them had not God held back the flow while they passed over. If they had attempted to walk through Jordan without the ark held in the midst, they would have been drowned in its waters. Therefore they had really crossed through waters of death as they passed over by faith to the promised land.

Spiritually, *Jordan represents Calvary*. The ark is the type of Christ. Just as the ark went first, and stood in Jordan while all the people passed over, so Christ carried the whole of His Church in Himself into the death of Calvary. The waters of judgment came upon Him as He hung upon that cross, and the whole Church of Christ was buried in Him, and, so to speak, "blotted out" in their connection with the fallen race of Adam—even as "all flesh" was "blotted out" by the waters of judgment at the Flood, when only Noah and his family escaped by being carried through the waters of death in an ark (Genesis 7:23, margin).

This crossing of Jordan is the most striking picture you can have of what it means to be crucified with Christ, and buried in His death. We were nailed to that cross in Him—identified with Him. We are thus buried into Jesus Christ, baptized into Christ (Romans 6:3–4), so that we may always look upon ourselves as buried in the Jordan; and once we have taken the position of faith in Him, crucified and buried in Him, the old life should not be dug up for examination, but always accounted as put out of sight and buried in the waters of death.

The two-fold aspect of our identification with Christ is portrayed by these two sets of stones. On the one hand, twelve stones were buried in the river flood, and on the other, twelve stones were taken from the riverbed and carried to the Canaan side as memorials of their separated life unto God. Similarly, we are taken into the death of our Lord and there buried so far as our relation to sin and to this world is concerned (Romans 6:1–13, Colossians 2:20 and 3:3), and out of that riverbed of death we are taken into His resurrection and triumphant life.

When the twelve stones were brought out of Jordan, they represented a new Israel. The old Israel was, in the purpose of God, left buried in the Jordan waters, and they rolled between them and the wilderness. The chosen people first crossed the Red Sea into the wilderness—this being the first stage of death on the cross, where the sea stood between them and Egypt. They were brought, so to speak, out of the world-sphere—Egypt—through the Red Sea into a new path, and then through the wilderness (a transit which should have lasted but a few months), and finally into Canaan— the land which is a picture of the heavenly sphere on earth, where the child of God is united with the Lord, a new creation in Him, and, having been equipped for war with the adversaries of God, is led forward by Him in victory. Let us now reaffirm *our* place in the Jordan, *i.e.*, in Christ's death on the cross. Retake the position there again and again, and say, "Now deeply buried in Jordan, buried in Jesus Christ on the cross, *I have died,* and I am buried out of sight. My Jordan—Christ's cruci-fixion—stands between me and the past, so I reckon that the past is gone, buried deep in the waters of death" (Romans 6:1–13).

Notice, too, that the priests went into the riverbed first, and there they stood. The priests represented the spiritual faith of the nation, and their position in the riverbed with the ark of God upon their shoulders indicated that the nation had taken its position of faith in the God who had bidden them cross that Jordan. After they *had* crossed they would never look back to the wilderness side of the river, but onward to the victory path ahead of them. Be-hind lay the river; in front lay the land which would become theirs in reality as they planted the foot of faith upon it.

When they went forward to the battlefield to take every inch of ground by faith, it would never have done for them to have kept saying, "*Did* I cross Jordan? Am I *sure* that I am out of the wilderness? I *feel* as if I was there still be-cause of the enemies here, and all these things to contend against. This must mean that I have never crossed out of the wilderness." But they *knew* that they had crossed Jordan, and just as certainly in your life you must stand on the fact that you *have been* brought through *your* Jordan—in Christ, in His death—on to the

Canaan side of Calvary, from whence you must pass on in the victory of faith to take the land!

But you say you do not *feel* it! Your feelings do not matter; it is the declaration of your position which counts. But you say that it looks as though there is still so much of the "old life" about you. Then *retake your position*, crucified and "buried with Christ" in the Jordan death of His cross, and count upon the Holy Spirit still more deeply to make it a fact in your practical life and give you keener insight to discern and cast off in quick obedience all that belongs to the past.

Look again at the way the Israelites crossed Jordan. They had no bridge! "Impossible," some might have said as they stood on the river's brink, and people say "impossible" now. Surely you do not get through to the heavenly (or spiritual) sphere simply by faith in Christ's death? Yes, you do! *No bridge*. That's right—no human way! There is no bridge which the human vision can see, but just a going down into the death of Christ by an act of choice and faith. By taking Christ's death as our own, and by the co-working of the Holy Spirit (Colossians 2:12), the child of God sinks down into Christ's death like the stones dropped down into the very center of Jordan, and from that fact the Spirit of God quickens the new life in Christ.

The new life *begins from the riverbed of death,*

just as the new nation—and then the new inheritance, gained through conflict—began for Israel; and the new life in Christ begins similarly for us, with its inheritance through war with opposing powers, its suffering and its triumph. All that was new to them began there, symbolized by the taking of twelve stones from Jordan and carrying them into the new life of the new land; and all that is new to us is pictured in the same symbol, as from henceforth we "reckon ourselves" not only "dead unto sin" but "alive unto God" (Romans 6:6, 10–11). Through the cross, identified with Christ into death, you come into union with Christ in life—and into the sphere where it is a forward march to take the land and to dislodge the enemy from every point. That is the other side of our identification with Christ, "alive unto God"; for the death-fact of our identification— being cut off from the past and reckoned dead indeed unto sin—is but the negative position, which now requires the *life* unto God as its power for continuance and for service unto Him.

Now comes the experiential part of the death-fellowship with Christ, as pictured in the story of Israel. After they passed through Jordan by faith and obedience there came the *real* application of the knife. At *Gilgal* the nation was circumcised, and they had to wait several days before going forward to the war as the

knife was applied to them. It was then also that
the man with the drawn sword was revealed
to Joshua outside Jericho. This suggestive part
of the story is true to fact in the spiritual life. In
this warfare with Satan, and with the enemies
of the Church of Christ, it is fatal for you to go
forward simply on the basis of *faith* that you
have died unless you let the Holy Spirit take
the *knife* and make a real severance between
you and sin and the world. That is to say, there
is a *real application of the severing power of the
cross,* which this part of Israel's history typi-
fies. When you have taken your position by
faith that you are buried in the Jordan waters,
you must be ready for the Holy Spirit to take
the knife and deal with whatever there may be
of the "flesh"* dominating your life. He will
bring about what Paul calls the "circumcision
of the heart," which is the true circumcision of
God.

Galatians 5:24 is also a passage which meets

* Weymouth has a note at Romans 7:18 on the scrip-
tural use of the word "flesh" which concisely
throws light upon it. He translates the word as
"lower self," and says it includes not simply the
body but also the mind, "in the degree in which
that consists of merely earthly thoughts, feelings,
affections, appetites and ambitions. The apostle
gives the name of 'flesh' to the whole of this earthly
nature, especially so long as it remains sinful, *i.e.,*
continues in rebellion against the higher nature,
which is its God-appointed ruler." Thus, from his

the case here: "They that are Christ's *have crucified the flesh* with the passions and the lusts thereof." This is judicially the position of all the children of God, but it must be so in actual experience also. For in this spiritual battle, unless the knife is applied to what the Scriptures term the "flesh," it will always be ground for the enemy to attack, so as to weaken us in the conflict. The "flesh" must be kept under the knife of the cross, for if there is any self-indulgence or anything that is doubtful in your life, and you venture to take the offensive against the foe, the enemy will come back on you, and—fastening on that uncrucified "ground" in you—will press against you with appalling power. You must have the knife of the cross *steadily, persistently,* and *unbrokenly* applied to the flesh: to the appetites of the flesh, to self-indulgence in any form, and to the pride of the flesh.

We have warnings of the need of the constant application of the cross around us on ev-

---

point of view, hatred, envy, bad temper, ill-natured talk, worldly ambition, pride, selfishness, self-righteousness, self-will, unbelieving and rebellious thoughts of God, a lack of industry, an indisposition to pray, deficiency in courage or straight-forwardness, all excessive social or domestic affections, all false patriotism, and all unhealthy curiosity and undue pursuit of knowledge are manifestations of the "flesh" or sinful earthly nature, equally with grosser and more animal indulgences.

ery hand. Have you not seen men spiritually sound in spirit one day, yet suddenly caught under strong delusion and led into fanaticism and wild extremes? You ask the cause. Down deep in the bottom of the life there must have been—for instance—some secret pride of the flesh uncrucified. They went forward into warfare against the enemy, and then there came upon them an evil spirit fastening on to that pride and manifesting itself as a spirit of delusion, leading these souls into a blind course of action until at last the poor deceived ones found themselves upon the rocks. *The knife must be taken to pride,* and to all other elements which make up the fallen Adam.

In this life of claiming victory, not only for yourself but for others, you must let the Spirit of God apply His knife to secret pride, secret ambition, secret self-assumption, and if you do not see its need just now, say to Him, "Lord, apply the knife of the cross to every bit of the old life in me, wherever Thou canst see it; in the places where I do not know it, especially down deep into secret pride."

Many shrink from the truth about the powers of darkness being able to deceive them, because of this hidden *pride.* They will not face the fact that *they* can be deceived, or caught by the roaring lion of hell. But one may ask whether God has given a special warrant that *you* in particular shall be free, and safe from the wiles of the devil. We must face it honestly and straightly, and own that we all stand in the same position in facing a wily foe. So it behooves us to walk softly, and to humbly ask God in His mercy to save us from any secret pride in our own strength of mind which will lead us to think of ourselves as so advanced spiritually that we will assuredly recognize the enemy and not be deceived by him in any way. Let us take care that there is no point where we get self-confident, so that the enemy traps us in the very place where we are off guard. Rather, let us take the position of prayer and watchfulness—willing to know the truth, without shrinking, about ourselves. Humility of spirit will place you where you cannot be hurt, and your feelings wounded, by anything said, because you desire only the truth, and do not care what it costs if you only find the truth as it is in the sight of God.

Then also let me say, it will not do for you to build on a past experience of the "cross." It is perfectly true that when you go into Jordan by faith you are to reckon that you are buried out of sight in its waters; but the fact that Israel afterwards had to submit to the knife showed that they had to experience the "cross" in a *personal* cutting of the flesh. So then, if you say regarding Galatians 5:24, "They that are Christ's *have* crucified the flesh; therefore there is no 'flesh' left for me to yet deal with," then you are just the one who can be trapped by the enemy, because you will not be counting upon the severing power of the cross of Christ in the present moment. It is only safe in this spiritual warfare to have a *present tense faith* in a *present tense application of the cross.*

You may have yielded to the cross up to the point of all that you knew last week, but there may be a hidden point in your character which the devil knows about and which you do not; and he is quietly fanning it up while you are off guard, thinking you are so "crucified" that he will never be able again to trap you. This is why souls are sometimes deceived and over-thrown in the very spot in which they think they are the strongest. *They are off guard,* thinking themselves so safe.

The wily foe can wait for twenty years, until he senses that you have forgotten all about something in your character—something which God dealt with so deeply that you thought you would never have to face the matter again. But now, twenty years afterwards, it is attacked by the enemy without your suspecting, and the occasion comes which causes you to discover that the devil is quietly aiming at the old place of weakness, and you have to vigorously say, "No! The matter has been settled and must never be debated again!"

Therefore you see it is one thing to say by *faith* that you have died to sin, and it is another thing to let God make it fact. When there comes the actual severance, then you know the knife. Keep this before you as you go forward into this battlefield. Pray the Lord to keep the knife of the cross applied to every part of your being, your *cleverness of intellect,* your *self-confidence,* your *sympathies,* your *affections.* Let the knife be used by God all the time, not yesterday but today. This means keeping the material which the enemy can fasten upon out of his way. The place of victory can only be known as the knife of the cross is kept continually applied to the old creation day by day.

After the application of the knife came the revelation of the Risen Christ: *"And it came to pass, when Joshua was by Jericho, that he lifted up his eyes and looked, and, behold, there stood a man over against him, with his sword drawn in his hand"* (Joshua 5:13). The battle was going to be the Lord's. Joshua was only the visible instrument; GOD WAS THE REAL LEADER. There He was with the drawn sword, ready for action. The war of God through Joshua was against the satanic hosts supporting the Canaanites. They dabbled with witchcraft and sorcery, and many had communion with familiar spirits; they were adept in the "black arts." The war was not with the Canaanites as men, *but with the satanic powers which they yielded to and worshiped in various ways.*

The Captain with the drawn sword implies

"war." Will you declare war too? Poor little frail mortal—what are you? Nothing! The power is with the Captain with the drawn sword. If you recognize Him as leading the war against sin and Satan, and all that Christ is at war with, you may be only a wisp of straw in yourself but you are one more who may, at least, be a block in the way of the devil. If you cannot speak, at least you can stand. You can put your foot down, and say, "I stand against everything that Jesus Christ is against; I do not know what that is, but I stand with the Victor with the drawn sword in His hand."

Now let us glance at some aspects of the war. Who would ever have dreamed of going to war to drive out the inhabitants of Canaan by first a simple march around the city of Jericho? What does this Jericho-victory teach us and typify? Jericho seems to be a picture of *prayer* victory. See the men of war walking round and round the city. An onlooker may say, "What silly people! Do they imagine that Jericho is going down by their simply walking around it?" Yes, there is an unknown power there. They are exercising *faith* in a Living God, Jehovah—the Lord of Hosts—and when the Captain with the drawn sword sees the invisible armies routed, He will say, "Shout," and down the walls will go.

But you must not shout until the Lord says "Shout." If we shout too soon, the enemy may gain an advantage. Sometimes we are so delighted when the walls of our "Jerichos" begin to move that we say too quickly, "The Jericho walls are down," when they have only just showed a sign of shaking—so we stop praying, and the enemy gains the ground. Far better to keep steady and quiet, lest we fail to pray through. A false idea of victory means that we are off guard before the victory is really won. Jericho seems to picture the prayer victory— that is, the assuming of a positive attitude of faith in relation to some great stronghold of the enemy which Jericho represents.

There is, however, another lesson—following the Jericho victory—which shows the need for a cool spirit and a sober mind when God answers our prayers and we learn the mighty power which faith has in pulling down the strongholds of the foe. This lesson is to be found in chapter 7:3, and may be called "the folly of *despising the enemy*," or the danger of being puffed up in the hour of victory.

Ai is only a little place. Not as many troops are called for at Ai as at the great city of Jericho. No need to send all the men of war there; just two or three thousand is enough. But *"the men fled before the men of Ai."* Here we see the folly of despising the enemy. When you understand the reality of this battle with the power of darkness, there will be nothing that is small to you. There are no "trifles" in this warfare. Every little point you must watch, else in the unprotected place—the matter you think too small to pray about—you may suffer a big defeat. This is the mistake many are making; either they despise the foe, or they magnify him and make him bigger than he is. *In no wise despise the enemy.*

Then notice the cause of the defeat at Ai. When Joshua cried unto the Lord he was told that there was a cause, and that cause had to be searched out. You know the story of Achan and the secret self-seeking which brought trouble to all Israel. It illustrates the need for the knife of the cross before we go forward to compass our "Jerichos" and capture our "Ais." In Achan's case it was the love of gold. There are "Achans" today in the Church of God who are grasping for gold and coveting beautiful garments, spending money on clothes while letting the "war" go forward without providing the money required for its progress. Take care, and watch lest you get defeated here even while you think you are walking in victory, for probably Achan had walked around Jericho with the rest! Examine the gold question, and the clothes question. Make sure that there is not even one point in your life that has not been brought into the light of the Lord Jesus Christ, and so act that you would be happy to give Him your bankbook to look at, and to hand over to Him to examine the expenditure for your home, and for your personal needs.

Now turn to the eighth chapter for a look at the lost ground of Ai, and the way to retake it as shown to Joshua by the Lord. Israel could not go any further into the land until they had gone back to Ai and obtained victory at the place of defeat. The Lord then used the tactics of the enemy to defeat the enemy; in the same way, every single advantage that the devil has gained upon you can be used in defeating him. You may be grieving over the fact that the enemy has deceived you, and that you can never be the same again; but the very advantage that the enemy has gained may become a weapon of victory, both for yourself and for others.

Remember that the blood of Jesus now speaks for you within the veil, and applied by the Spirit of God, it cleanses from all sin. Counting upon the precious blood to cleanse, now say, "Lord, make use of that net of the devil's to give me light as to how to rescue others." The experience you have gained becomes then a stewardship which you are responsible to use for the deliverance of others. Cease to grieve over the past, and use your testimony for the salvation of others. Do not let pride hold you back. Admit that you were deceived, and testify as to how you were set free, so that other souls may beware of Satan's wiles through what has happened to you. Do not "save face" at the cost of letting others go unwarned and undelivered. Make no excuses, even though you *were* "honest and true." There are other souls besides you who were honest and true, who have been sidetracked by the enemy.

The Lord told Joshua to go back and attack Ai. You cannot go any further until you have regained lost ground. That which is right in your path must be overcome. How often we shrink back, unwilling to face up to the lost "Ais," until at last we say, "Lord, in Thy grace and strength, whatever it costs, I will retake the ground I have lost." The Lord will not lead you to any other victory until you have won the "Ais" right in your path.

Are you determined to be on the side of King Jesus, and to engage in war against the principalities and powers in the heavenly places? And, under the Captain with the drawn sword, will you be strong and of good courage today? Will you set your face to victory on the basis of Calvary and advance against the foe? Will you let the Lord apply the knife to everything in you and about you that the enemy can use and can fasten upon to paralyze you? And will you in God's name determine that every place that the sole of your foot shall tread upon shall be yours?

You are in a mission hall, for instance, and have given your witness there, but the people will not hear it. The enemy says, "Leave them."

But *stay* there, *stay*, and hold your ground. "They won't let me speak!" Then *pray!* Hold the ground by prayer, until the Lord drives out all hindrances to His working.

Is there a certain point in your life where you always fail? Be determined in Christ's name that that piece of ground shall be held for Jesus Christ. *Hold the ground,* and be of good courage.

You can see that though the enemy does beat you back and does gain an advantage, as he did at Ai, and you have fled before him, you *have to go back to your lost position* before you can advance one step more. It is an awful thing to turn your back to the enemy, and to let the powers of darkness drive you back from an advanced position that God has given you. When you have put your foot down for God upon any ground, *hold it,* and let nothing draw you away from any place that God has given you, even though you wait many years until you see the visible answer.

If you put your foot down to take a certain place by prayer, hold on until the place is won. In the children of God who truly stand on the Canaan side of Jordan there is a divine resistance to the spiritual foe, given of God, that says, "I would like peace, but they—the powers of darkness—are for war. *Therefore, I am for war too*—war in the name of Jesus Christ, to dislodge the forces of Satan from their strongholds."

The horizon is full of light and victory and triumph, and of the possible glorious liberation of all the people of God who have got entangled with the powers of darkness. Keep your eye upon the Risen Lord. The Captain with the drawn sword has never lost a battle yet, and He is going to lead the Church of Jesus Christ to battle now. The call is ringing out, "Rise, children of God, in the name of the Conqueror, rise! In the name of the Christ of Calvary, rise!" The Captain is going to lead to victory; keep your eye on Him only. You have your foot on a piece of ground? Stand there, and do not try to collect the scattered soldiers. Stand, let the Lord rally them; but stand where you have put your foot, on the furthest point He has led you to, and you shall come right through to victory in His name.

2

Retaken ground—the javelin of faith—be-
ware of snares—testing the guidance—the
"Waterloo" experience in Canaan—the battle
of the five kings—put your feet upon their
necks—the righteousness of God.

WE have already had, in some degree, a
glimpse into the war in Canaan. Here is
the chapter outline: chapter one, the leader's
preparation; chapter two, the commission and
the spies; chapters three and four, the way to
the battlefield, over Jordan; chapter five, the
knife, as preparation for conflict; the end of
chapter five, the Captain with a drawn sword;
chapter six, the first stage of the war, Jericho as

a picture of prayer-victory; chapter seven, the folly of despising the enemy, defeat and its cause; chapter eight, retaken ground. Now we will again deal with the last subject—retaken ground.

"*The LORD said unto Joshua, Fear not, neither be thou dismayed: take all the people of war with thee, and arise, go up to Ai. See, I have given into thy hand the king of Ai, and his people, and his city, and his land; and thou shalt do to Ai and her king as thou didst unto Jericho and her king. . . . So Joshua arose, and all the people of war, to go up to Ai: and Joshua chose out thirty thousand men, the mighty men of valor, and sent them forth by night. And he commanded them, saying, Behold, ye shall lie in ambush against the city. . . . And it shall be, when ye have seized upon the city, that ye shall set the city on fire; according to the word of the LORD shall ye do: see, I have commanded you. And Joshua sent them forth*" (Joshua 8:1–9).*

The 18th and 26th verses of the same chapter show what Joshua himself had to do while the men of war went forward to retake the lost ground of Ai.

"*The LORD said unto Joshua, Stretch out the javelin that is in thy hand toward Ai; for I will give it into thy hand. And Joshua stretched out the javelin that was in his hand toward the city. . . . For Joshua drew not back his hand, wherewith he stretched out the javelin, until he had utterly destroyed all the inhabitants of Ai.*"

All that Joshua did was to stretch his hand

out, and KEEP IT OUT until the entire city was taken.

Notice here the combination of faith and action. The warriors had to engage in actual fighting, but Joshua had to take the faith-position of *keeping his hand stretched out.* How strange these ways of gaining victory in the Old Testament! Moses on the hillside lifting his hands, and now Joshua stretching out his hand while Israel went forward to take the city. Elisha, in his day, told the king to strike an arrow on the ground, and when he struck three times he told him he had settled the limit of his victory, and would get victory three times and no more. These pictures of faith and action are very remarkable and seem to show the leaders and prophets as DEALING WITH THE INVISIBLE FORCES, while the rank and file went to the actual war.

The power over the invisible forces of evil lies in the ATTITUDE OF FAITH, and if you are not able to go down to the battlefield you can in your own room take the attitude of victory, stretching out the javelin by faith for others in the front of the battle with sin and Satan. That is what the Church needs now—the children of God so knowing God that they will hold the victory of Calvary for the deliverance and triumph of the Church of God. Yes, in faith standing in victory while others are going forward into active service. And *both*—the one exercising the faith-attitude and the other going forth to the battle—are reckoned equally "in the war" by the Lord. David seems to have understood this principle in spiritual things, for he said, "He that goeth forth into the battle and he that tarrieth by the baggage shall share and share alike" (1 Samuel 30:24, paraphrased).

This combination of faith and action, pictured and shown to be practical and effectual, as seen in the Old Testament, must be WORKABLE NOW. Those who go to the mission field should have those at home who can stretch out the "javelin" of faith on their behalf, holding the attitude of victory over every specific phase of conflict in the mission field until it is through. Joshua's faith-javelin was behind the men of war until they regained the lost ground. You can thus take an attitude in your will, simply saying, "I stand with God for victory there, and there, and there," and quietly settle down to hold it, until the ground is taken for the Lord. There must not be a looking at appearances or difficulties, but a tenacious faith that the invisible principalities and powers must give way before the believer stretching out by faith the "javelin," thus indicating the conquering, overmastering power of God.

Where are the possible places of lost ground in this present time? For instance, there are some persons out of their old sphere of work. You say to them, "I thought you were ministering in such and such mission hall." "Yes, well—there was opposition. I gave up for the sake of peace!" That is *lost ground.* You should have held your position in the teeth of opposition until the Lord gave His own peace—the peace of victory. You must now go back and hold that ground. How? By PRAYER. If you cannot go in person, there is a sure route another way. You must retake that ground in the name of the Lord, *in prayer,* and claim the victory for that place.

Any ground that has once been taken for God must not be given up by you. The Lord will point out to you men and women all the different ways in which this will apply to your lives. Is the Lord indicating to you any lost ground in any aggressive warfare for Him? Have you failed to hold any place you once took for Him? Have you had your "witness" silenced, and your work checked? It may have been the lack of the outstretched javelin of faith over the invisible forces in the air, a weapon you have failed to wield, and so you have been driven from or hindered in your work by the wily foe.

God wants His witnesses everywhere; and every piece of ground held by those witnesses for Him belongs to Him and must be held on His behalf by continuous acts of faith. There is a retaking of the ground. I know of a child of God on the committee of a Free Library for the selection of books. She has been a true witness for God there, by her voice raised against the admittance of books with poisonous error in them, and she has had a hard battle to hold her ground. She has been attacked in every possible way, but the Lord has stood with her. This is what He wants today—WITNESSES who will not be silent and let the god of this world have his way. May the Lord give you courage to hold your ground where He has put you.

As we pass on to chapter nine, the word is *"Beware of snares."* Suspect everything in the time of battle!

"It came to pass, when all the kings that were beyond the Jordan, in the hill-country . . . heard thereof, they gathered themselves together to fight with Joshua and with Israel with one accord. But when the inhabitants of Gibeon heard what Joshua had done unto Jericho and to Ai, they also did work wilily, and went and made as if they had been ambassadors, and took old sacks upon their asses, and wine-skins, old and rent and bound up, and old and patched shoes upon their feet, and old garments upon them; and all the bread of their provision was dry and was become moldy" (Joshua 9:1–5).

And Joshua was deceived!

"The men took of their provision, and asked not counsel at the mouth of the LORD. And Joshua made peace with them, and made a covenant with them, to let them live. . . . And it came to pass at the end of three days . . . they heard that they were their neighbors, and that they dwelt among them" (vv. 14–16).

So they gained a covenant of life, when God had commanded their death; and they obtained by *strategy* permission to live! Here are the snares.

Joshua was deceived by appearances. Beware of the snares hidden behind appearances. *Suspect everything.* But you say, "How can you live like that?" It only means take nothing for granted in this spiritual warfare, and test everything that comes to you either from the supernatural or natural realm around you. How? For instance, suppose I say to you, *"Refuse all suffering which comes from the devil!"* You reply, "How are we to know it is from the devil?" Test it by the declaration of your attitude. Say, "If this is suffering given me from God, I take it; but if it is from the devil, I refuse it. Now let God settle which it is." If it is from the enemy, it will pass away as you maintain the attitude of refusal. If God has some lesson in it to teach you, it will remain. Every single thing you must test. Suspect everything, for the enemy will imitate everything, and all day long will watch to get you to make a "covenant of peace" with him and to let him alone. Therefore, over everything say, "What is of God, I take; what is of Satan, I refuse. Now let God prove which is which." Or, in other language, "refuse" everything that comes from Satan and "choose" everything that comes from God, by the simple declaration of your refusal and choice, as occasion arises hour by hour.* For you must not imagine that you will be able to discern the source of everything with the first look, for the deceiver can so hide himself and work under cover that in most cases you cannot detect his presence or his devices at once—you can only apply a test, and know by the results of the testing.

Suppose you are very, very tired. You say, "How am I to know whether the enemy is putting such pressure on me that I cannot do the work or whether it is simply ordinary fatigue?" In reality it is quite simple, if you understand that your will—your choice—is the deciding factor. Say, "If it is from the enemy, I refuse it; if from natural causes, and I really need rest, I accept it. Now, Lord, prove which is which." If it is from the enemy, as you declare your attitude of resistance to him you will find it will pass away, and you will say, "I thought I was quite unfit to go on, but I find I am all right!" God will prove which is which, in the way of the supernatural cause, as you exercise your

---

* This simple attitude of the will as the deciding factor of the soul in yielding either to God or the devil has been well understood in relation to temptation, but not so clearly in relation to the workings of Satan as a Deceiver—seeking all day long to mislead the believer; as a Hinderer—seeking to hinder when he cannot do more; as a Murderer—seeking to injure and even kill God's servants; and in every other aspect of his workings.

choice. As you set yourself on God's side against the enemy, the enemy will flee, over and over again (James 4:7).

Suppose you find hindrances in the way of your going to a meeting? How can you know whether it is God who wants you to stay away or whether it is the enemy trying to hinder? *How* can you know? Again just say, "If the Lord does not want me to go, I choose to stay; if the devil wants to hinder me, then Lord, I ask You to destroy his works. Remove the obstacles and open the way." In brief, let me say again, test everything, and *declare your choice* about everything, every step of the way—while you also count upon the blood of the Lamb as your ground of victory (Revelation 12:11).

In this part of the warfare you must ask the Lord to give you keen power of recognition. And always give God time to work for you. Joshua was in too much of a hurry. Even Joshua who had been guided and taught of the Lord was deceived by the enemy. Therefore you cannot say that you are absolutely safe from his wiles. In times of uncertainty—*wait*. Always, if you have any doubt, *wait*. Do not force yourself to any action. If you have a restraint in your spirit, wait until all is clear, and do not go against it.

One tactic of the enemy is to get you to *hurry in your decisions,* so that you fail to decide in accordance with the mind of God. You must "catch the outgoing mail." Your correspondent must have an answer by tomorrow morning! Yet you have not had time really to pray and make sure of the will of God. Far better to wait. Refuse to be *pushed* to a hasty or doubtful decision. Do not write until you are clear! But is it not very discourteous? Better to be thought discourteous than to act without the assurance of God's will. To escape the wiles of the devil, walk in quiet, steady soberness, and *suspect everything* enough to make you test every step of the path hour by hour. In brief, "*Watch* and pray."

As you walk in the path of the cross, and maintain in faith and practice the death-position to sin and the world, the Spirit of the Lord will give you power to see and to understand His way. May I give you an example of how God thus teaches His children, from my own experience? I can recognize now how twenty years ago, when I first knew the leading of the Spirit of God and His guidance step by step, the devil tried to insert his misleadings to confuse me in guidance. I recollect sitting with my Bible in front of me and asking the Lord for guidance whether I should go to one place or another. I opened the Bible, and my eyes fell on a text which I thought I ought to take as "guidance." I was very perplexed, for the text was very indefinite, and I could not see what it meant; yet I tried to think it out and to obey it. I went to the place I thought the text indicated, but there was no result such as I expected. Then I saw that there was something wrong in this vague way of guidance; it is not the way the Holy Spirit leads. My mind was happily awake, and reasoned, "It is not like the *Holy Spirit* to give me guidance to do a thing, and when I obey, to find there is no purpose in it." I never went by haphazard "texts" again. To be misled once in such a way is enough! If I had followed on in this course, and not learned by the first lesson, the enemy, as an angel of light, would have misled me like many others who have been sadly mistaken in more crucial things; but, by the mercy of God, I was enabled to refuse, from that day forward, acting upon isolated texts.

That manifest attempt of the false angel of light to mislead me enabled me at once to discern how the enemy is watching to mislead the surrendered children of God, and to discover how the Lord really works. The enemy would have liked to get me to follow his "will-o'-the-wisp," but I kept steadily to the path of the cross, asking the Lord continually to expose the enemy as I went forward, bent upon doing the will of God.

You say, "Will not such a watchful attitude make you very miserable?" No. It simply reminds you that you are in the enemy's country, and that he is always on the watch to ensnare you; and it moves you to alertness in asking the Lord to open your eyes and expose him.

God led me also, some fifteen years ago, into contact with certain souls, purposing to teach me the wiles of the enemy; I could have written a book then about those wiles and the need of knowing in deep reality the power and shelter of the cross. And the experience of all the years that have followed has taught me that one safeguard against the devices of the enemy lies in knowing the cross. This has been confirmed again and again by others, and only recently by a worker who has proved it while passing through very subtle workings of the devil in the way of deception in the things of God. She said the one thing that had saved her was her knowledge of the crucified life in the fellowship of the cross, for she clung right through to the fact of her death with Christ; and as she held it, the Spirit of the Lord brought her into clear vision and complete deliverance.

We will now look at chapter 10, the story of the battle with the five kings who combined and came up against Israel. The progress of the war in Canaan is very suggestive. In one chapter it is Jericho—a city. In the next, it is the attack on what we would call a village. Then we have the taking of that village. Next comes the story of the snares of the enemy. And here in chapter 10 you have a big pitched battle against five kings—a "Waterloo," so to speak, in the history of the taking of Canaan, when several kings joined together to fight against Israel.

Before Israel went forward to the battle the Lord said to Joshua, in the eighth verse, *"Fear them not: for I have delivered them into thy hands."* He might have replied to the Lord, "It does not look like it! How I wish You would send an angel from heaven to prove it!" "No, no, Joshua, you must take My word, and go forward to the fight, and *then you will prove it."* *"Fear not,* I HAVE . . ." said the Lord. Not fighting to get victory, but *in the faith* that he *had got* the victory, Joshua had to go forward—and you, too, must go forward, because the word of the Lord has said so. You do not have to "*get* the victory," but to fight from the *position* of victory, and thus get a manifestation of it!

Joshua then came upon these kings suddenly (v. 9), and the Lord discomfited them before Israel and slew them with a great slaughter; *"and it came to pass that they fled before Israel"* (v. 11); *"and Joshua returned, and all Israel with him, unto the camp to Gilgal"* (v. 15)— the place of circumcision, you recollect, before they attacked Jericho. "And these five kings fled, and hid themselves in the cave at Makkedah. And it was told Joshua, saying, The five kings are found" (vv. 16–17). That is just like the satanic enemy we fight against; his "world-rulers"—his "kings" or "principalities"—know well how to hide in "caves." They get into places where you cannot find them. Then Joshua said, "Roll great stones unto the mouth of the cave, and set men by it to keep them; . . . pursue after your enemies" (vv. 18–19). Yes, you may have to shut up some of the enemy by prayer and roll stones to the cave for the time being, in some attack upon you, because it may not be the moment for dislodging and dealing with that particular enemy.

We are in a great warfare, and the prince of darkness is actively at work; we have had to focus prayer upon shutting up some of his emissaries for a time, and to "put a stone on the cave" where they are hidden, while we deal with other foes attacking or fleeing yonder. Joshua bade Israel pursue after the fleeing enemies with bold and confident words—"The LORD your God *hath delivered them* into your hand" (v. 19). His was the voice persistently declaring the *victory* promised by God. THAT, TOO, WILL MAKE YOU A LEADER, for it is the business of a "leader" to keep telling the armed men of war that God has given the victory, until the spirit of it gets into the soldiers in the ranks who have to prosecute the war.

Thus Joshua said, ". . . Stay not ye; pursue after your enemies and smite . . . them; suffer them not to enter into their cities, for the LORD your God *hath* delivered them into your hand."

So, "it came to pass, when Joshua and the children of Israel had made an end of slaying them, . . . all the people returned to the camp . . . in peace: *none moved his tongue against any of the children of Israel*" (vv. 20–21). Thus also can the children of God who know how to affirm the victory of Christ over Satan at Calvary close the mouth of the devil. But they must not run about from one to the other, passing on tales themselves, and feeding the devil's fires; for then they become a mouth-piece for the enemy and will not be able to close his mouth against the people of God. If, however, you yourself have learned the mastery over their devices to make *you* speak over-much, you can ask the Lord to "suffer not the demons to speak" when they seek to hinder the work of God by using the mouths of God's children. The Lord would not allow a dog to "wag his tongue" against His people when they came out of Egypt; and here in the story of the conquest of Canaan, we are told that none of the Canaanites "moved his tongue" against the children of Israel.

Then said Joshua, "Open the mouth of the cave, and bring forth those five kings" (v. 22). And they "brought forth those five kings," and when they brought them forth, Joshua said unto the chiefs of the men of war:

"Come near, put your feet upon the necks of

these kings. And they came near, and put their feet upon the necks of them. And Joshua said unto them, Fear not, nor be dismayed; be strong and of good courage: for thus shall the LORD do to all your enemies against whom ye fight" (vv. 24–25).

Joshua needed to get the chiefs to understand how absolutely fearless they must be, and so he brought them into close quarters with the enemy. And Jesus, as if He were saying "Come, put your feet on them," spoke likewise to His disciples: "Behold, I have given you AUTHORITY TO TREAD upon serpents and scorpions, and over all the power of the enemy; and nothing shall in any wise hurt you" (Luke 10:19). *Put your feet on their necks!* But you must bring them out first. There are hidden enemies, as it were, in a "cave" in your life; you must bring them out and face them. If you have things that you are terrified of, ask the Lord to bring them out so that you may look at them. Do not be afraid of anything, but let everything come out. Ask the Lord to expose all the hidden workings of the adversary—to bring him out of his hiding places—and then put your feet upon him; *"and the God of peace shall bruise Satan under your feet shortly"* (Romans 16:20).

One hard lesson to learn is how to put our feet on the enemy. I remember fifteen years ago how hard it was to learn it. It necessitated going through one of the great conflicts of my life, but the Lord had to teach me again and again to win the victory over Satan, until I became fearless against him. It came about in this way: I was seeking to help a soul who was terribly misled by the enemy. I did not know then what I do now, and I tried every way I could to get her free, but it was in vain—except for intermittent periods of time. The foe tried to make me afraid; but I realized that one shade of fear would mean that he would conquer me. I understood very little about warfare with Satan, but I knew intuitively that I must be absolutely fearless, and maintain *in spirit* a fearless attitude toward him. I often went then from awful conflict with the power of Satan in her straight on to the platform to speak, with scarcely time to open the Bible to get a message. How often my hearers used to say, "How is it God blesses the message?" but they little knew where I had won my victory before I went to them.

This soul I had to bear with year after year, refusing to deliver myself, as I very easily could have done . . . but God was with me, and answered me again and again as I cried unto Him. One day, for instance, I went to the Lord and said, "If this poor soul is doing something I ought to know, please bring it to light." That night she put a letter into my hand, saying, "Read that!" And I found that she had given me a letter written to another which told me all she was doing.

In those days I was learning the Lamb-spirit of Jesus, and I thought if I only had the "Lamb-spirit" she would see it, and I should win her that way. But to my amazement she got worse and worse. I thought the "Lamb-spirit" of Jesus always conquered, but it seemed to me that the more I showed it, the more the devil mastered her and conquered. At last I went to the Lord and asked Him to show me what to do, and this was the answer: "*Put your foot upon* the necks of the five kings!" But I shrank from "putting my foot down," and would so much rather that she should have her foot upon me. "*Put your foot down!*" But it is easier to be a lamb than to put the foot down. "*Put your foot down!*" was the only message, and I knew that obedience was the only way to victory. So when that soul came to me again, instead of listening to her with a smile, as if she had done nothing wrong, I said, "God has shown me that I must not any more 'smile' upon you, until you have repented and put away all that you are doing wrong. This is the last time I dare overlook and ignore what you are doing, because I see that the devil is getting a greater hold on you through my forbearance." From that hour I had to stand firm as a rock, refusing to act as if it was all right when I knew she had not put away all that was wrong in her life. I told the Lord that was the hardest thing He had ever given me to do, but I never knew the righteousness of God until that hour.

THE LOVE OF GOD! Yes, I thought "love" was to overcome everything—but I then saw that *righteousness* was true love, for the love of God could not injure the loved ones by overlooking sin. I saw that the "Lamb-spirit" had been used by the enemy to make her bolder in wrongdoing, and I had to learn how to resist him in the *righteousness* of God. My Bible became so alight with the righteousness of God that its words cut like a knife. It seemed as if God kept saying, "I cannot compromise with sin, and you must stand against sin; for if you smile on that sin, I hold you to be a partner with it." I saw that I was never to compromise with sin by being silent on it or *appearing not to notice it* when I knew a soul was wrong. I understood 1 Samuel 15:29–33, and similar texts, as never before, and realized that I must stand with God against sin and be faithful against it at every cost.

When you have learned the spirit of the Lamb, and find it easier to *yield* than to rebuke, the hardest thing for you to do is to put your foot down; *but you must do it.* God holds you responsible. You must ask God to bring the "kings" of the enemy out for you, and then you must put your foot down upon their necks.

Yes, when once you have learned the Lamb-spirit of Jesus, the hardest thing in this whole world is to carry out the righteousness of God. If you have not learned the Lamb-spirit, then the flesh can be very righteous and very hard; but if you have learned it, then your heart will be very broken with love for sinners while you stand with God in righteousness against what they are doing wrong. This is the only way that we can be witnesses for God today. It is "preachers of righteousness" that He and the world need.

For this cause, children of God, you need to beware of any "supernatural experiences" which *dull your sense of right and wrong, and render you less acute in spirit and mind to recognize right and wrong.* Your growth in the knowledge of the Lord Jesus Christ is really manifested by a deepening and more acute sense of what is right and wrong, rather than in ecstatic experiences. As you grow in the knowledge of Christ there will come into the very depth of your being an undeviating principle of action which will say not "Do I *like* this?" nor "Do I *feel* that?" but *"Is it right?"* If a thing is right, you must do it; and if it is wrong, then you must die rather than do it. In this warfare it is righteousness that counts, for it is a warfare between the God of Righteousness and the prince of wickedness—it is a battle between righteousness and sin, where your "feelings" must not be considered.

Since the experience I have named, the righteousness of God has been more beautiful to me, and I would rather that my God should be righteous than even that He should be loving. I could not worship a God that was not righteous. If my God tolerated sin, and smoothed it over, I could not worship Him.

If there is anything about your life that is not in accordance with the righteousness of the Holy One, then let Him deal with it—for His righteousness is highest love. In this warfare you must have nothing to do with what to *you* is wrong. Do not ask other people what is right or wrong, but ask God to make you *know* what is right or wrong for *you*; and THEN BE TRUE. Do not give what "so-and-so says" as a reason for any course you take, but do what *God* has shown you is right, up to the fullest knowledge of your light obtained from the Word of God; and then "happy is he that condemneth not himself in that thing which he alloweth" (Romans 14:22, KJV). Be true! Never mind experiences, *be true!* Be true, and do *right for right's sake*, not because it benefits you and makes you happy. Be right because it is right, and because God is holy! Amen.

3

The cause of the war in Canaan—the extent of the destruction—the danger of being ensnared—four ways of being ensnared—the accursed bar of gold—the bedrock position of victory for the spiritual warfare—the declared attitude against sin and Satan.

LET US now consider what was the cause of the war in Canaan, and why it was to be so terribly exterminating. In Deuteronomy 7:2, we read that when Israel was preparing to go into the land, and Moses spoke of the Lord delivering up the nations of Canaan before them, he said, "Thou shalt smite them, then *thou shalt utterly destroy them;* thou shalt make *no covenant* with them *nor show mercy* unto them." The cause of this terrible, merciless extermination we are shown in Deuteronomy 9:4–5, "Speak not thou in thine heart, after that the LORD thy God hath *thrust them out* from before thee, saying, For my righteousness the LORD hath brought me in to possess this land; whereas FOR THE WICKEDNESS OF THESE NATIONS THE LORD DOTH DRIVE THEM OUT FROM BEFORE THEE. Not for thy righteousness, or for the uprightness of thine heart, dost thou go in to possess their land; but *for the wickedness of these nations the LORD thy God doth drive them out from before thee!*"

The words here are alive with new meaning, as we read in the light of present conflict with the forces of darkness and the war against them in the heavenly places, the words—*"drive them out," "thrust them out,"* "The LORD thy God doth *drive them out,"* and then the expression *"I thrust them out from before thee!"* The Israelites *were a factor in it.* They were not going to sit down on the edge of Jordan while the Lord did it without them, but *He* would thrust the enemies out before them. They had to be the *instruments* with which GOD would drive out the foe.

"The Lord thy God shall thrust them out" is the word for you also in the present battle. You have to march forward in His victory, and He will thrust them out! Would that the Church of

God understood this and knew how to rise to the place of victory in the victory of the ascended Lord! Would that she understood that the Lord our God could *drive out the powers of darkness* in front of the Church of Jesus Christ as the nations were driven out before Israel!*

Then notice it was not for the "righteousness" of Israel that these nations were to be driven out; not because they were such a "perfect" people, or perfect weapons for God. You say, "Look at my failings; look at what I am. I cannot fight in this warfare. If I were absolutely perfect, I could expect the Lord to use me!" But it is not because of your righteousness the Lord is going to drive out the powers of darkness before you. It is the righteousness of Jesus Christ, who is "The Lord our Righteousness"—it is the victory of the Christ of Calvary.

Let us turn again to Deuteronomy 7:2. I wish to emphasize the attitude which Israel had to take towards these nations of Canaan. Look how strong the language is: "Thou shalt smite

---

* And they *will be driven out of the heavenly sphere* when the Church of Christ is caught away to join the Risen Head. As the Church ascends to His Throne, the prince of darkness and his angels will be cast down to the earth, preparatory to the then-nearing hour for the binding of Satan and casting him into the pit. See Revelation 12:5–12 and Revelation 20:2–4.

them; thou shalt *utterly destroy* them." In the margin we find a strange word in this connection—the word "devote": "Thou shalt utterly *devote* them." They had to be devoted, or handed over to death without flinching— "Thou shalt make *no covenant with them,* nor show mercy."

In the fifth verse will be seen the reason for this attitude also to the religious rites of these nations: "Thus shall ye deal with them: ye shall *break down their altars.*" Their religion—which meant communion with satanic powers—had to be dealt with, equally without mercy: *"Dash in pieces their pillars"*—their religious pillars— "HEW DOWN THEIR ASHERIM, AND BURN THEIR GRAVEN IMAGES WITH FIRE." Such was to be the attitude of Israel to the idolatry of Canaan, which had at the back of it the worship of demons. There was to be absolutely no compromise, no covenant, no mercy. The words are so strong that, if they dealt only with the human side of things, they would appear beyond reason; but all is clearly understood when you see God dealing with that which lay at the back of the religious rites of Canaan—SATANIC POWER. Paul makes this plain in the First Epistle to the Corinthians, where he says an idol in itself is "nothing in the world," but it is the demon at the back of the idol (1 Corinthians 8:4; 10:19–20).

God's war in Canaan was with Satan and

his hosts, for the religion of the Canaanites was simply satanic worship. Everything spoke of communication with satanic powers. The land was swamped with what we could sum up today in the word "spiritism," so the attitude of people representing the Holy God was to be without mercy. "The graven images of their gods shall ye burn with fire . . . for *they are an abomination to the* LORD *thy God;* neither shall thou bring an abomination into thine house, and become a devoted thing like unto it: thou shalt *utterly detest it*, and thou shalt *utterly abhor it;* for it is a devoted thing" (Deuteronomy 7:25–26).

We need to pick out the words from these sentences so that they stand out with striking force, and thus get them into both ears and hearts, for they mark out for us what is to be our attitude today to the powers of darkness, and the prince of darkness—our attitude to everything that is touched by satanic power. Our attitude today is to be the same as God's attitude to these satanic hosts at the back of Canaan's wickedness.

THE WAR WAS WITH THE GODS OF CANAAN. Their altars were to be broken, their pillars dashed; and it was not to be done, as one would say, with kid-glove delicacy; it was not to be done superficially. The words "hew down," "burn," "utterly detest," and "utterly abhor" express forceful action. Look at the language, and see how it reveals God's hatred toward all these wicked, fiendish, rebellious hosts of the heavens—Satan's principalities and powers.

There must come into us, also, some understanding of God's hatred and judgment and curse on the devil's forces, expressed in the commands to Israel as to their attitude to the nations of Canaan given up to the worship of these fallen, invisible ranks of heaven. It is the curse of Eden being carried out: "The LORD God said unto the serpent, *Cursed art thou*"; and everyone that will identify himself with, and touch the things of the serpent, that curse must come on him. "Keep yourselves from the accursed thing, lest ye make *yourselves* accursed," warned Joshua (Joshua 6:18, KJV). What is the attitude of the Church of Jesus Christ today to satanic spiritism, and all other manifestations of satanic powers, in the light of these words to Israel?

Again, if we turn to Deuteronomy 12 we shall see another reason why Israel was commanded to take such a strong attitude toward the nations in Canaan. The danger was, lest they should themselves be ensnared! God had to bid His servant Moses use this strong language to make Israel understand His abomination and hatred of sin, and the "wickednesses which are spirits" (see Ephesians 6:12), so that they might be protected in Canaan from any contact with, and the consequent ensnaring by, the supernatural evil powers they would meet in the land. God had to put a gulf of *death* between Israel and the satanic wickedness of Canaan.

A glimpse is given in Deuteronomy 12 of ways in which they could be ensnared, and the solemn warning was given, "Take heed to thyself, that thou be not ensnared to follow them" (v. 30). The same solemn warning is needed today, for even Christians—professing Christians—are trifling with God by tampering with spiritism and other demonistic "isms" of these perilous times. There is a seeking to familiar spirits today which is certain to call down the severe judgment of God upon those who do it, for God is at war with these things now as much as He was with the Canaanites.

How many professing Christians are dabbling with spiritualism? How many with the doctrines of demons that are sweeping in on every side? Did we ever know England as it is today? We have never known our sober-minded, quiet, well-balanced England swept, and tossed, and driven about by all kinds of the strangest, wildest doctrines of demons such as we find now. God's children are such cowards, they do not want to know these things. "Let us have our nice little meetings and pray," they say, "but do not tell us these things. They make us very uncomfortable!" Soldiers of Jesus

Christ not wanting to know about the enemy! They fear lest too much is said about the devil! If the prince of darkness would leave us alone, we would leave him alone; but until he ceases to attack the Church of Christ, God's servants must speak against him as well as against all unrighteousness.

If God had to exterminate the Canaanites because of their dealing with familiar spirits, their sorcery, witchcraft and idolatry, it is surely certain that judgment is coming upon spiritism and the satanic things of today. God was at war with Canaan because of what we would describe today as "spiritism"—dealing with the supernatural evil powers. It is time that the Church should wake up to see that God is at war with all that is of Satan—with what is now sweeping over the land where the gospel is already known *but not obeyed*. It is time for God's children to take heed to what they are doing, to be careful what they are teaching and what they are reading; for there is literature being scattered everywhere which is full of the most subtle teachings of deceiving spirits, literature which has hidden in it in germ the very abominations of Canaan which drew down the judgments of God.

"Take heed to thyself that thou be not ensnared to follow them . . . and that thou inquire not after their gods, saying, How . . . ?" The Israelites were guarded by being bidden not even to *in-*

quire after the things which the Canaanites worshiped. It is best not to *read* books about Theosophy and other cults of today, which prove they are not of God by their toning down of sin and their attitude against the gospel of the cross of Christ as the atonement for sin; for the subtle poison of the evil spirits behind the words gets into the mind of the reader, and it is not easily removed. The Lord did not tell Joshua to read all the books of the sorcerers and mediums of Satan in Canaan so that he might know how to deal with them, but He told him to *meditate day and night upon the Law of the Lord.*

Alas, the need of this saying is great! Children of God following on to know the Lord are drawn into reading these books full of subtle poison, thinking their *minds* are able to judge them. Then they say, "I have been reading a book, and all my difficulties are solved—wonderful views of God's ways, all the puzzling texts explained," and so on, *not realizing they have come into contact with a spirit*—the spirit of error. They are also not trained enough in the Word of God to detect the poisonous words— error which renders *inoperative* the truth— which are wrapped up in ninety-nine words of *truth*. Thus the subtle foe is at work today, hiding his baits in bushels of words so that it is difficult to find them. How different it is with God, for when He sends His message to a dying world He puts it in simple language so that one can understand it; but the devil pours out, through those whose minds are perverted, such torrents of words—ofttimes beautiful— that you cannot find out where the error is. Beware of a jumble of words, and juggling with God's Book—the Book which the enemy is working to nullify on every side in these days.

One way Israel could be ensnared was by "inquiring." Oh, children of God, keep to your Bibles! Keep to the simple truths of God's Word! One startling danger upon us today is how little *the Word of God* is known by Christians. They can give strings of favorite texts, but as to telling you intelligently the fundamental, straightforward truth of God, they are dependent upon others for that. Those who take God's Book and read it throughout—Gospels *and Epistles*—until it is incorporated in their very innermost life, will quickly realize when what they hear is out of line with that Word, and they will not be drawn away from the truth as it is in Jesus.

"If there arise in the midst of thee a prophet, or a dreamer of dreams, and he give thee a sign or a wonder, and the sign or the wonder come to pass whereof he spake unto thee, saying, Let us go after other gods, which thou hast not known, and let us serve them; thou shalt not harken unto the words of that prophet, or unto that dreamer of dreams, for the LORD your God proveth you, to know whether ye love the LORD your God with all

*your heart and with all your soul. . . . And that
prophet, or that dreamer of dreams, shall be put to death,
because he hath spoken rebellion against the LORD your
God . . . to draw thee aside out of the way"* (Deuteronomy 13:1–5).

Here we read that a "sign" or a "wonder"
coming to pass when foretold by a "prophet"
is *no proof that he, or it, is from God.* The ultimate
test is the result of the "sign" and not the sign
itself. Does the sign lead you away from God
to contact with other "gods" or objects of worship? That is the point. *Where does it lead to?*—
that is the proof. The test is so plain. God knew
that there were supernatural powers in Canaan
and that there would be dreamers of dreams
and prophets arising, moved by Satan, to draw
the people away from the Lord.

We can see clearly by this statement from
God that a sign or a wonder coming to pass is
no proof that it is of God, yet it is on this point
that many are led astray. They imagine that if a
thing comes to pass, the proof of its being of
God is beyond question; but the believer must
discern more carefully what is the effect of this
or that upon him in his spiritual life. Where
does the "sign" or the "wonder" lead? Does it
lead you *nearer to God,* and nearer to His children? *Does it tend to unite or disunite the people of
God?* Does it make you more loyal to God or
lead to the worship of "other gods"—even in
the sense of placing your "experience" as of

greater value than the bare word of God? In this supernatural warfare, take heed, and recognize that signs and wonders are no proof that a "prophet" or a "teacher" is of God; nor does the fact of their predictions being fulfilled bear witness that they are of God.

In verses 6–8 of this chapter we read again, "If thy brother . . . or thy son or thy daughter, or thy wife . . . or thy friend that is as thine own soul, entice thee secretly, saying, Let us go and serve other gods, . . . thou shalt not consent." Here is the snare to a believer through family ties. The nearest and dearest may be the instruments used by the Canaan enemies to reach the loyal Israelite, but all must be resisted that draws from God—even though the temptation comes from those who are as "thine own soul."

There are four things, therefore, referred to whereby the Israelite might be ensnared: *by inquiring; by wonders*—through prophet and dreamer; *by family or friend,* drawing one aside; and then in Deuteronomy 13:12–15, we find pictured the snare of *public opinion,* as follows:

"If thou shalt hear tell concerning one of thy cities, which the LORD *thy God giveth thee to dwell there, . . ." that they "have drawn away the inhabitants of their city, saying, Let us go and serve other gods which ye have not known, then shalt thou inquire, and make search, and ask diligently; and, behold, if it be truth, and the thing certain, that such abomination is*

wrought in the midst of thee, thou shalt surely smite the
inhabitants of that city with the edge of the sword."

These are four possible spheres of danger
needing watchful care on the part of a loyal
soul. You may escape being ensnared by obedience to the command not to "inquire" into or
touch the things filled with satanic guile; you
may escape the snare of being drawn aside by
any supernatural "sign" or "wonder"; you may
escape by faithfully resisting the influence of
your dear ones, when they seek to draw you
aside; and yet you may fail by going with the
multitude when it comes to the question of
public opinion. If everybody says a thing, then
it *must* be right, for "The voice of the people is
the voice of God!" The voice of the people was
not the voice of God at Calvary! It was the *voice*
of the devil. When the deceiver fails to get hold
of you, when you stand true even if your dearest friend leaves you, then when it comes to
public opinion and the multitude—the whole of
your city or country—*then* can you stand?

But you have to stand true to God through
it all.

Notice also in the four sections of danger,
God's remedy for dealing with the enemy's
work is "death" and "fire." What is the spiritual meaning of these terms? *Just Calvary's*
death for you. You must take the attitude of
death and declare, "I have died with Christ";
then there will be the gulf of death between

you and all these things. And *fire!* This is the burning up of all that can be burnt in your life; but your own attitude can only be death—even the death of Calvary.*

Let us pass on to Deuteronomy 18:9–15 before we go to the conditions of victory and mastery. "When thou art come into the land which the LORD thy God *giveth* thee. . . ." Yes, you do not go into the "heavenly places" because of "your own righteousness," but as the result of the righteousness of the Lord Jesus. It is the "land which the LORD thy God *giveth* thee," and He gives it *before* you enter in—gives it to you in Christ. It is only when you go in that you see the dangers there. These dangers were not in the wilderness. There it was hungering after the flesh pots of Egypt. The "powers of darkness" let them alone there, for their fleshly cravings made it unnecessary for Satan to show his hand, as in Canaan. In those who "walk after the flesh," the devil needs only to let the "flesh" work—while he keeps out of sight. But when God's people cross the Jordan and get into the spiritual realm on the resurrection side of Calvary, then they need to be awake to the additional snares. Even so, the Lord will drive out the enemy before them on the condition of the absolute separation of death between the child of God and the world.

* See Galatians 6:14: "Crucified . . . unto the world."

"When thou art come into the land which the LORD thy God giveth thee, thou shalt not learn to do after the abominations of those nations. There shall not be found with thee any one that maketh his son or his daughter to pass through the fire, one that useth divination" (Deuteronomy 18:9–10).

What is divination? Do you remember that Paul was followed by a girl that had a spirit of divination (Acts 16:16)? This is simply the satanic counterfeit of the power of the Holy Spirit. It is written in John 14:26 and John 16:13, "The Holy Spirit shall teach you all things . . . and He shall declare unto you the things that are to come." We have promised to us the true, deep, inward teaching of the Holy Spirit to be the indwelling, resident power in our spirits, making us know the things of God (1 Corinthians 2:10). But "divination" is the satanic counterfeit of this divine knowledge, given by a "spirit of divination."

Do you say that has nothing to do with you? Do not be too sure. Satan can counterfeit the Holy Spirit and make you know, and tell you things, so that you cannot detect which is which by your own insight. In this passage you have it expressed clearly that the "abominations" of the nations of Canaan were bound up with the work of evil spirits, for they used "divination" such as that described in Acts 16—when Paul cast out the spirit from the girl possessed with the "spirit of divination." That evil spirits can speak the truth when it suits them we find by this spirit saying, *"These men are servants of the Most High God, who proclaim unto you the way of salvation."* All this was true, and Paul might have said, "What a testimony that we are the servants of God!" But Paul would not accept the testimony of evil spirits to his apostleship. Had he done so, the power of God in him would have been identified with the power of evil spirits, and he knew he had enough testimony to the divine character of his work in the salvation of souls through him. By this we learn that we do not need "supernatural" testimony to our work, and that the best testimony that God is with us is that God saves and blesses others.

The spirit of divination is the counterfeit of the work of the Holy Spirit.

"There shall not be found with thee any one that . . . practiceth augury . . . or a charmer, or a consulter with a familiar spirit, or a wizard, or a necromancer. For whosoever doeth these things is an abomination unto the LORD, and because of these abominations the LORD thy God doth drive them out" (Deuteronomy 18:10–12).

Do you see here what God's attitude is towards all the working of Satan and his counterfeits? The whole war of Canaan is summed up here: "BECAUSE OF THESE ABOMINATIONS the LORD thy God doth drive them out." God's war was not with flesh and blood, but with the satanic things. Jericho must have been full of them, as the chief city of the nation. Canaan was full of them—altars, idols, obelisks, and all kinds of things, evidence that the prince of darkness held the land, and that the inhabitants were soaked in supernatural evil powers by yielding themselves to divination and familiar spirits. In that one statement you have the true cause of the war with Canaan.

We can see now why the Book of Joshua is said to be the Old Testament foreshadowing of Ephesians. What lessons there are for us as we understand God's war with the principalities and powers of Satan.

Now let us consider the conditions given personally to Israel for mastery over the inhabitants of the land, apart from the actual war upon them. In Deuteronomy 11:8–9, we read, *"Ye shall keep all the commandment which I command thee this day, that ye may be strong, and go in and possess the land."*

The first condition of equipment for mastery was implicit obedience to the Word of God. This again shows you the importance of feeding on God's Word and seeking to have it so dwelling in you that your spirit is made strong. "Keep *all of the commandment* . . . that ye may be strong, and go in to possess the land." Implicit obedience to the full command of God—that they were absolutely not to tamper with nor touch the things forbidden by

God. To see this more clearly we will again go to the story of Jericho.

The Lord said about Jericho, *"The city shall be devoted"* (Joshua 6:17). In the margin it says "accursed," or in effect, "devoted to the curse." In Eden, God pronounced a curse upon Satan; this brought a curse upon all who identified or yielded themselves to him. The city of Jericho was "devoted" or given up as under "curse," for in Jericho there was a gathering up of the abominations of Canaan, which, we have seen, were "abominations" because they were inspired and controlled by the hosts of hell.

"You *must keep yourselves from the devoted thing,"* said Jehovah (verse 18). The Lord made it emphatically wrong, so that no one marching round the city of Jericho should take a thing connected with the city—thus paralyzing all Israel by having had contact with the accursed things of Satan, and coming under the curse upon him.

They were to "keep themselves" from the accursed thing. Ah, you say the *Lord* has to keep *you!* But *you have got to keep yourself too,* for the Lord will not work a miracle to prevent you taking hold of a thing He forbids. You must not place on the Lord what He expects you to do for yourself. "He that was begotten of God keepeth himself, and that wicked one toucheth him not" (1 John 5:18). Because the Lord undertakes to keep, *you,* as a responsible being, must keep yourself by not touching the accursed thing, "lest, when ye have taken of the devoted thing, ye make the camp of Israel *accursed.*" How solemn this is. The curse that is on the devil will come on God's people if they utilize things that have their source from Satan, and hence have his power upon them.

What is the secret of victory? *Absolute separation.* Which way? First by the death of Calvary—which we shall consider later on—and by *obedience to the command of God.*

Now if you look at Joshua 7:4, you will see how Israel knew when the "curse" had come upon the camp. The city of Jericho had been taken, and all seemed to be going well when the men of war went to Ai—about three thousand of them—but they fled before the people of Ai. They ran because they had lost the power to stand—to be aggressive and to fight. Neither Joshua nor any of them knew that the curse had come on the camp *until they went up to war.* Then their splendid "men of war," fresh from the conquest of Jericho, ran away. They turned their backs before the enemy, and *then* they knew something was wrong. *Had God failed?*

Even Joshua did not know that the curse had come. He saw the defeat and cried, *"We must have more power"*; and he went and flung himself down before the Lord, and said, "Alas, O Lord GOD, wherefore hast Thou at all brought this people over the Jordan, to deliver us into the hands of the Amorites, to cause us to perish? . . . Oh, Lord, what shall I say, after that Israel hath turned their backs before their enemies!" (Joshua 7:7–8).

Was it "more power" that was needed?

The Lord said, *"Get thee up; wherefore art thou thus fallen upon thy face? Israel hath sinned . . . they have even taken of the devoted thing. . . . Therefore the children of Israel cannot stand before their enemies; they turn their backs . . . because they are become accursed"* (vv. 10–12). Why? What is the matter? How had they become "accursed"? Was it only a little bar of gold?

We have heard sermons about this. We have talked about the gold and the clothes, and we have thought that *they* were the "accursed things"; but the gold in itself was right, and the clothes were right. What then was the matter with them? They had the "curse" on them! They could be clean if they were God's, but they had the curse of God on them because God's curse was on the satanic powers that held the city and the land. It is not the exterior things: it is not the piece of gold; it is not the garment. It is the power *at the back of them*, soiling and stamping them, so that if you appropriate anything that belongs to the "god of this world," it brings the curse on you and on the camp.

As a sequel to this Achan story, we see once more how radical had to be the work of separation from contact with the enemy's cursed things. *Death* and *fire* were the only way for Israel. The solemn warnings of God had to be carried out. Death—spiritually applied to us it means the death of Calvary—and fire, the destruction of fire, alone could purify God's army once again.

Joshua knew that they had lost the co-working power of God against the enemy only when they went to war and found that they were without power to conquer or to stand. And so it is in the spiritual conflict today. Yes, every step of the Canaan victory came through war—by taking the *offensive* against the foe. And so it is today. What does it mean to "take the offensive"? Must you go out to the street corner and preach? That is only the exterior and material side. The inside truth means that in your spirit you are always taking the attitude of aggressive victory against Satan and all his hosts, wherever they are. "Is that all?" you say. But that is much. *In your spirit,* mark you! What you may do outwardly is another matter; the Lord will show you His will on those points. But in your room at home you can take an attitude of aggressive opposition in spirit, and say, "Lord, in Thy mighty victory I take the offensive in Thy name against all the hosts of darkness that are pressing down on the work of God in China, Korea, India or Africa; and whatever Thy people are standing against, I stand with them, in the name of Jesus Christ."

How is this possible? Because in the spirit the whole Church of Christ is one, and if you are joined to the Living, the Risen, the Ascended Christ in the ascended life, those Christians in China, or Korea, or India, or Africa are also members of the Body; and if one member suffers all members suffer. You need to recognize the oneness of the Body of Christ, and that you are as near to that other member of the Body in China, "in Christ," as you are to those who are near you here.

For this aggressive warfare in spirit against the powers of darkness you need to hold persistently the death-attitude of Romans 6. You declare that you stand in death to the world and all that the god of this world brings; death to the desires of the flesh, that they do not master you. Then as you walk in the Spirit, you will not fulfill the lusts of the flesh. You can declare death, not only to the world and all the things of the flesh, but death also to the powers of darkness, giving them no right to you, as one who is in Jesus Christ—hidden in Him— refusing them any admittance, or control, or right, or power over you. This is your fighting position, and your footing for continual victory.

Before we move on to a further aspect of the

cause of the war in Canaan, and the purpose of Christ's death on Calvary, let me again make very clear that the one bedrock position for maintained victory over the power of the enemy is found in Romans 6. You may have known this long ago, and let it slip in the stress of the conflict. Let us clearly understand that the "old creation"—or the first-Adam life—is material for Satan to work upon. The "old creation" was identified with Christ on the cross of Calvary (Romans 6:6). In Romans 6 Paul sets forth the complete, finished work of Christ, when He carried sins, *and the sinner,* to the tree. Your footing for victory is not your *experience* of this but *what Christ has already done,* applied to you by the Holy Spirit.

If our victory depended upon the measure of our experience of it, then some of God's children would have to say that, as they did not yet personally grasp it all, they could not get victory until, say, "next year." We would be resting on our personal experience, and not on *the finished work of Christ.* It is not what Christ has done *in* you, but what He has done *for* you on the cross that is the standard of deliverance. What He did *for* you was that He carried the old creation to the cross, and our old man was crucified with Him.

The "god of this world" is holding everything around you. The god of this world is permeating everything, covering everything in a thick, impenetrable darkness, and inducing blindness. If you are going to be a warrior in aggressive warfare, knowing that God is with you and that God will drive in front of you the powers of darkness, you must be in a position of death to the world. "Far be it from me to glory, save in the cross of our Lord Jesus Christ, through which the world hath been crucified unto me, and I unto the world" (Galatians 6:14). Here Paul declares his death-attitude to the world.

Your position for Canaan victory in the heavenly places is that you say steadily, "I declare death between me and the god of this world, and all the things he touches." There must be the separation of death. Romans 6 is like the Jordan line of separation between the wilderness and victory. Romans 6 means the death-separation between the earthly and the heavenly sphere. Romans 6 is *Calvary*. It is the place where the death of the cross comes between you and everything. It is the one bedrock position which represents Jordan in New Testament language. The stones buried in the waters of that stream correspond to the statement "we have been buried with Him by baptism unto His death." Buried stones in Jordan; buried Christians in Christ's death.

Now it is for you to take the entire finished work of Christ by faith, and count upon the Spirit of God to work it out. Then when you meet Satan, or have conflict with the enemy, you are to appropriate *at that moment* the entire finished work of Christ. As you stand on that finished work, the Holy Spirit applies it to you in its full power, and Satan is defeated. He will have to fall off from you, and retire, while you abide hidden in the Christ of Calvary.

It is not well to go much into detail, but there are some spiritual experiences which you cannot tell quickly whether they are of God or of the devil. This, however, is the way to test: just say, "Lord, I stand on Romans 6 and all that it means just now. Make it into fact." This has been verified by souls who thought that certain supernatural experiences they were having were from God; they ceased in a moment with the appropriation of "Romans 6" and never came again.

Hold that death-position strong and clear, and do not reckon it is an attitude of yesterday but of the present moment. And do not be confused by the experiential side of it. God will make it personal as you stand on the finished work of Christ. Say, "Romans 6 and all it means," and the Spirit of God will apply it.

This death is to be a perpetual attitude of reckoning. It must be the first thing in the morning, and right on through the day. You must stand unshaken on Calvary's death-ground—death between you and everything around you that you are not to touch; then in union with the Risen Lord you must go on and declare war against the powers of darkness. Yes, you must take the *offensive* in the spiritual sphere in order to remain in it unbrokenly.

The Lord said to Israel, "I have given you the land, and *every place that the sole of your foot shall tread upon,* to you have I given it" (Joshua 1:3). The danger when you have your footing on Romans 6 is that you could become passive, thinking that "death" means passivity, *i.e.,* that because you are in the attitude of death you are not to act, and not to go on and do anything! But PASSIVITY IN A SPHERE WHERE THE SPIRITUAL ENEMY IS ACTIVE IS FATAL. Therefore, while you declare your position in Christ's death, you must also take the offensive against the enemy, in the activity of the spiritual power of life unto God.

When the enemy attacks you, and tries to drive you into yourself and cause you to say "I am only this and that, and the other," the best answer is, "I resist you [James 4:7]; in the name of Jesus Christ—depart." And when he leaves, you will find all the tossing and tumult about yourself will cease. Then you will say with wonder, "It is peace."

Do you know how to "fight" the foe with Romans 6 as your fighting position? When you go to take a meeting, for instance, do you say, "Now, Lord, I stand on Romans 6, and standing here, I claim Thy victory over all the powers of darkness that may hinder me here"? In like manner you can take the aggressive attitude for your home as well as for your meeting. The first thing in the morning you can say, "I take a position against all the powers of darkness that try to work in this house today. I stand against them in the name of the Lord."

May God awake and arouse His Church to see that if she will only take her place first in His Calvary-death—the place of the buried stones in Jordan—then, in the name of the Mighty God of Hosts, and under the leading of the Captain of the Lord's Hosts (whom Joshua represented at Jericho), in His name she can dare all the time, in spirit, to take the offensive against the powers of darkness around her. THE POWER OF ATTITUDE IS MORE THAN WE KNOW, and if you just say, "I stand *against* the powers of darkness—I am *against* the workings of the enemy," the Lord your God will surely drive them out before you, even as He promised.

Shall He drive them out of that mission where you are working? What are the conditions? That you do not touch any part of the accursed thing, *i.e.,* things with the touch of Satan upon them. I cannot tell you in detail what these are, and you do not need to be concerned about them in detail until occasion arises; simply take the attitude that you do not intend to touch, and you will not touch. Say, "I declare the position of death between me and the things of the powers of darkness, in all that they bring to me, and in all that are around me," and stand quietly there. It is an attitude of spirit only, but it *works* in practice, as many have proved.

How striking is the great weakness of many of God's children! Their natural strength is no good here. It goes under like crumbling clay. Many are running away from conflict; they are terrified at the word "conflict." Where are the souls that will stand?—souls that will say, "If I cannot do anything else, I can *stand*"? That is all! Only *stand*—stand where you are put. Stand in victory for that mission. Stand in victory for that church. Stand in victory for the servants of God everywhere.

God could awaken the whole Church of Christ if His servants only knew these things— if they really understood that in Jesus Christ they have a right to silence the devil and not let him speak to them when he brings his evil suggestions to their minds. Oh for souls who will say, "In the name of Jesus, be silent! You have no right to speak to me, for I am Christ's!"

When you see gossip in your church, do you add to it? Someone has lit the enemy's fire, and he is using Christians to feed it. In the name of God, just go quietly to your room and say, "In the name of Jesus Christ I command these evil spirits to stop their use of the Christians' mouths."

Will you ask the Holy Spirit to open your eyes to this vital aggressive warfare against the prince of the power of the air, and ask God mightily to strengthen your spirit to take a strong, resisting attitude to all his hosts? Read the passages we have referred to, and then say, "I utterly detest them, I utterly abhor them, and I will break down their altars and hew down their pillars." And keep asserting this in the name of Jesus, so that the accursed thing may be driven out of the camp of Israel. But you must also say, "I will not have gold at the price of anybody's blood and suffering." *This is the gold with the curse upon it.* "I will not have gold that comes unrighteously." *This is the gold that comes with the curse on it.* You need not get into bondage about it, but just declare in the name of Jesus that, as far as you have *choice* about it, the gulf of Christ's death shall be between you and the things that Satan instigates. Declare your attitude to these things, and then the curse shall not come upon the camp, and you will be able to stand in front of your enemies. There must be no running away from your mission because you are slighted there; no running away from your church because you do not get what you wish there. You will say, "I stand here, and I will hold my ground and not turn my back before the enemy's driving out—but in the name of the Lord God,

Satan's deceiving spirits shall be driven out from this place for His glory."

Will you say, "I stand on Romans 6, and in the name of Jesus I count on the Lord of Hosts driving them out before me"? In the name of Jesus drive the enemy out so that your home may be sweet; in the name of Jesus drive them out of that drunken woman, drive them out wherever they are, in front of you, as you claim the victory of the Risen Lord!

"The eternal God is thy dwelling place, and underneath are the everlasting arms. And He thrust out the enemy from before thee, and said, Destroy" (Deuteronomy 33:27).

4

The curse in Eden — the curse on Canaan — the curse of the broken law — the curse on Him who bore the curse at Calvary — the curse of God declared by His representatives — the curse by Deborah — by Elisha — by Jeremiah — by Malachi — the curse usable in prayer as shown by Christ — the "let him be accursed" by Paul — no more curse.

WE have already seen why the destruction of the Canaanites was to be so merciless. Brief reference has been made to the fact that Jericho was the accursed city, and that any of the Israelites taking anything in that city came under the curse that belonged to it. Now I wish to enlarge upon that thought, and from it proceed to show you what is meant by our Lord Jesus Christ bearing the curse on Calvary. Christ has indeed borne the curse for us, but in order to get a clear understanding of that far-reaching truth one needs to compare scripture with scripture. With this in view, we will turn first of all to the curse of Eden, as given in Genesis 3:14: "The LORD God said to the serpent, Because thou hast done this, cursed art thou above all cattle."

The order of God's dealing with Adam and Eve and the serpent is worthy of notice. First, He spoke to Adam: "The LORD God called to the man, and said unto him, Where art thou?" Second, He called to the woman: "The LORD God said unto the woman, What is this thou hast done?" Third, He turned to the serpent as the first cause of sin, and declared, "Cursed art thou." This interrogating order was reversed when God pronounced judgment upon them. First the judgment was upon the serpent, who was cursed as the first cause, and the first in order; then God turned to the woman, and although she had been deceived, she was told she could not escape the consequent suffering; and lastly the man was told, "With the sweat of thy brow shalt thou eat bread." The order in which God addresses the three—first the man, then the woman, then the serpent—and the reversal of it in the pronouncement of judgment—first the serpent, then the woman, then the man—is very remarkable and suggestive.

It is equally remarkable to notice that because the woman was deceived by Satan, and was not a willful transgressor, she was chosen as the means of his defeat. Paul points out in his first letter to Timothy that Adam's transgression was *willful,* that is, fully knowing he was doing wrong, and that there would be resulting consequences; he was not therefore chosen for the undoing of the serpent's work, but was given the part of toiling at the cursed ground for material sustenance. The woman, who had been deceived innocently, was chosen to produce the promised Seed which would bring about the absolute defeat of Satan.

In this we may learn the lesson that God will turn the very devices the enemy uses against His children into weapons for his defeat. Willful transgression brings the judgment of God upon it, even though the transgressor is forgiven; but every single thing in which Satan may have deceived you, as an innocent victim of his wiles, can become the very cause of his defeat. May God give you that comfort through this glimpse into the fall in Eden—especially those of God's children who have been deceived by "supernatural manifestations" which they afterwards found were not of God, and who have fallen into depression, darkness and despair.

Eve was innocently deceived by the serpent, and then in His grace God promised that *through her* would come *the very defeat of the one who had deceived her*. Yes, God can turn the very devices of the enemy into a weapon of victory over him.

Again, in your past life you may have taken some step which you afterwards discovered was the result of deception in guidance. You thought you were doing the will of God, but later you found that you had been misled by the enemy. Be of good comfort; God can lead you back into His safe pathways, and He can use that very misleading for greater personal safety, and effective service.

I have in mind a true servant of God who is now in bitterness and darkness because some years ago he believed that God planned to use him in a special way for some great blessing in the mission hall in which he was a worker. Alas, the enemy sidetracked him; and today he is in darkness, grieving that he missed the will and purpose of God in his life at that time. Children of God, do not grieve over any step which you now think to have been out of the will of God in past years. If you acted honestly, truly, sincerely believing that you were really following the Lord, and it was not until afterwards you found out that it was not the Spirit of God at all but a deceiving spirit of Satan—

instead of giving way to despair and depression, just take comfort that God will use you on that particular point to defeat the devil in his attempt to mislead others. When I learn from a soul of any such deception, and of the doubt and conflict which Satan brings to them as a result of it, how thankfully I tell that soul that the very point of deception will become a weapon for use against the deceiver in helping other souls out of danger. Here you have it in the Scriptures: Eve deceived, and then chosen to be the mother of the Seed that would bruise the serpent's head.

Yes, every single thing in the past, where you have been honest and true and sincere, and yet *misled by the enemy*, can be turned to his defeat. (See, for example, Luke 22:31–32.)

Now let us look at the curse which God pronounced in Eden. The Lord said to Adam, "Cursed is the ground for thy sake." The curse was pronounced upon the serpent, and also upon the ground. If we turn to Genesis 8:21 we shall find a precious word in regard to the latter, where we see that, when Noah came to the new world—carried to it in an ark upon the waters of judgment—the Lord took away the curse from the ground. When Noah came out of the ark he built an altar, and it is written that "the LORD smelled the sweet savor; and the LORD said in His heart, I will not again curse the ground any more for man's sake, for that the imagination of man's heart is evil from his youth; neither will I again smite any more everything living, as I have done." So apparently, in the new world, clothed with beautiful fresh verdure and brightness, the curse on the earth itself was removed.

Then there comes a painful story, in Genesis 9:25, of what happened in the new world to the very one who had led his family out of the old into the ark. Noah was drunk, and when he came out of his drunkenness, he said, *"Cursed be Canaan."* Into the ark with Noah had gone his three sons, Shem, Ham, Japheth— and Canaan was the son of Ham and the grandson of Noah. In one of the Minor Prophets there is a sly reference to Canaan as a "trafficker" (Hosea 12:7, see margin) in whose hands are "the balances of deceit"; this may show that Canaan had something to do with the disgraceful condition of Noah, and that Ham "abetted."* In Habakkuk 2:15, we read also, "Woe unto him that giveth his neighbor drink . . . and maketh him drunken also, that thou mayest look upon their nakedness!" This verse seems to refer back to the episode connected with Noah and his son and grandson. When we take both passages together, along with the action of the sobered Noah toward his grandson Canaan, it seems clearly to show that, in some way, Noah was deceived into the con-

---

* *The Midnight Cry*, E. McHardie, page 65.

dition he fell into. Eve was deceived in Eden by the serpent; and now once more the archenemy of God and man gained a fresh advantage on the newly cleansed earth by deceiving, through the agency of someone in his family, the man who was the head of the new government.

The curse came upon Canaan—the deceiver—and *through him upon the Canaanites,* who afterwards were to be driven out of Canaan by the Israelites: "Canaan begat Zidon his firstborn, and Heth, and the Jebusite, and the Amorite, and the Girgashite, and the Hivite, and the Arkite, and the Sinite, and the Arvadite, and the Zemarite, and the Hamathite: and afterward were the families of the Canaanite spread abroad" (Genesis 10:15–18).

Here we see the history of the enemies of Israel, the Canaanites—who came under the curse declared on Canaan by his grandfather Noah. Noah the patriarch was the head of God's new government for the new world, cleansed by the flood. Canaan, his grandson, apparently led him to drink, and when he came to himself, by the Spirit of God he pronounced the curse, declared to be on the serpent, as *now coming upon Canaan;* and from and through Canaan's descendants came the entry of the satanic forces in rampant power throughout the world. Or, we may say, that in the new world after the flood, Ham and his son Canaan became the channel for the working out through men of the curse pronounced on the serpent, and on all who identify themselves with him by yielding to him to carry out his will.*

The curse upon Satan has never been taken away. The curse that came upon the Canaanites was the result of their being given up to satanic powers, right from the time that Canaan had the curse pronounced upon him by Noah. Hence the condition of the Canaanitish races in the days of Joshua, who was commanded to drive them out from Canaan. The satanic powers worked in them, and through them, from the days of their forefather Canaan.

Turning from the history of Ham and Canaan, with their descendants occupying Canaan, we may trace the line of the godly seed of Shem, and find them gathered together at Sinai where God gives them the law as a nation. Afterwards we find Moses commanded to recite to them the *curse* that would come upon *them* if they broke that law; and THAT CURSE HAS NEVER BEEN LIFTED. It runs in a continuous line with the curses that precede it—first, the curse pronounced upon Satan; then, the curse running into the Canaanitish races,

---

* The curse had been originally pronounced on the serpent, and now by identifying themselves with him, they became liable to the curse in all its force. *The Midnight Cry.*

and manifested through their sorceries and spiritualism; and finally, the curse of the law to be realized in Israel's disobedience, pronounced when God took the godly line of Shem and, gathering them at Sinai where the law of the Lord was given, rehearsed through Moses those awful curses upon all who broke His law (Deuteronomy 27–29).

We find, therefore, three sets of "curses" in operation in the world: (1) the curse on Satan pronounced in Eden, and never annulled; (2) the curse on the Canaanites through their forefather Canaan, bringing upon them the judgment through Israel; and (3) the curse on all who broke the law of God given at Sinai— which abides, as we shall see further on, until this day.

To the curse on the devil we say, "Amen, so be it"—may it be carried out to its end. To the curse of God upon all the works of Satan, manifested through all who identify themselves with Satan by dealings with familiar spirits, again we say, "Amen." But there is the curse of God *upon all who break His law*—what shall we say to that? As you read these curses as set forth in Deuteronomy, you will do well to study them in the light of the speaker's entire message. Moses, representing God, had to stand before Israel and pronounce God's curse upon all who broke the law given through him at Sinai. Neither during that period of 1,500 years of Old Testament history which follows the events of Sinai, nor in any other period since—apart from the finished work of Calvary—has that curse ever been lifted. That "curse" stands today, as it stood in the days of the Apostle Paul, who wrote to the Galatians (ch. 3:10): "For AS MANY as are of the works of the law are under a curse: for it is written, Cursed is every one who continueth not in all things that are written in the Book of the Law, to do them."

In this passage we come further down the centuries and nearer to ourselves than Sinai. Note that the apostle writes, "AS MANY as are of the works of the law," *i.e.,* as many as rely upon their keeping of the law of God, "are UNDER A CURSE, for cursed is every one who continueth not in all things that are written in the Book of the Law, to do them." Is there a soul who will rise and say that he keeps absolutely, without one jot or tittle being broken, all God's law given at Sinai? If not, you are under the curse of that broken law, as stated in Deuteronomy 27. This was the way Paul brought souls to see their need of Jesus Christ, through conviction of the curse of the broken law.

In relation to these words, Paul says that God "shut up all . . . under sin" (Galatians 3:22), so that no one can find a way of escape which will enable him to say that he is not a sinner. James says if we offend in one point we are guilty of all, so that one single point of the broken law brings us under the curse of the law. What hope is there for Jew or Gentile? For Paul's readers or for us? Here Calvary comes in—God's remedy. The apostle wrote, "CHRIST REDEEMED US FROM THE CURSE OF THE LAW, HAVING BECOME A CURSE FOR US; for it is written, Cursed is every one that hangeth on a tree"—referring to Deuteronomy 21:22–23.

Really? Are *all* who do not accept the Lord Jesus Christ as their substitute under the curse of the law? Christ was made a curse for us on Calvary's tree, but the curse on Satan remains, and the curse of the broken law on all who stand on their obedience to it remains. BUT THE CURSE IS REMOVED AT CALVARY FOR ALL WHO WILL ACCEPT THE SUBSTITUTE PROVIDED BY GOD. Calvary is the one and only spot where we get away from the curse of God. *There is no curse there.* You escape the curse of Satan, and the curse on sin—you escape in Jesus Christ.

You escape the curse of the broken law upon you by believing into Jesus Christ—*into* Jesus Christ, buried with Him, planted into Him, put into Him. Outside of Him you are under the curse of the law; in Him you are free from the curse—for the curse was on Him. Deeper still than this do the words "Cursed is he that hangeth on a tree" carry us, for they show us how the curse came upon the old creation. Will you say "Amen" to that curse upon the old creation which Christ carried to the cross? He bore the curse for us—even God's curse of the broken law which was upon Him—and in Him alone you are free from it. Christ was made a curse for us, and all are under the curse except those who are in Jesus Christ—planted in Him! The way to personal freedom from the curse upon sin is, of course, by our identification with Him who bore the curse of sin, as we reckon His death ours; and we obtain a victory over Satan and his power, just as the Israelites did at Jericho, by not touching the "accursed thing."

Have you ever taken the position that is yours in Christ towards Satan, and his accursed doings, in which you may ask God to fulfill His curse upon them? When Satan attacks you, *you may remind him that God's curse is upon him,* and he will flee away. Do not forget that which is written about the serpent: "The LORD God said, Cursed art thou."

Let us turn to instances in the Bible where we may see clearly how God's servants, as His representatives, pronounced or declared the curse of God upon all actions that bore upon them the marks of the work of the enemy. First of all, there was Noah. When Noah awakened and found out what was done unto him, he said, "Cursed be Canaan," thus voicing the curse of God upon Canaan's deception of him, because its source was Satan. If you are "joined to the Lord" and truly standing with Him, and in Him, against the powers of darkness—if you deeply realize that God's curse is upon sin and Satan—you can, as united to Jesus Christ, voice His attitude to both.

Then we find Moses, the man of God, declaring God's curse on all who broke the law of God, because he stood as God's representative against sin.

Then there is Deborah! What did she mean when she sang, *"Curse ye Meroz, said the angel of the LORD.* Curse ye bitterly the inhabitants thereof, because they came not to the help of the LORD, to the help of the LORD against the mighty" (Judges 5:23). We read that Deborah "judged Israel" at that time (Judges 4:4), and the men of Israel went up to her for judgment, because they saw that she had spiritual insight and discernment given to her of God. Why did she speak such words about Meroz? Because she saw that those in Meroz were taking the *side of Satan*—the god of this world who is at the back of all sin and wrong—and she was only the voice to declare that "the angel of the LORD" had said that the curse would come on them; because by their apathy and inactivity in a time of crisis for Israel they had practically taken sides with Satan, and not with God. It did not mean that *Deborah* "cursed" Meroz, but her utterance was the result of her spiritual insight, for she saw what is really true also today, that in a time of crisis for country or Church, neutrality is not possible; that holding back from "taking sides" when enemies are at hand is a selfish apathy which can only be instigated by Satan, and hence it must bring upon the souls who do it the curse belonging to Satan.

Because these "leaders" stood with God in righteousness, they had the view of God upon the real causes of things and, of course, saw and spoke from God's standpoint. Noah foretold the curse coming on Canaan—carried out in truth by Israel; Moses had been shown in the Mount by God Himself that all who broke the law would come under the curse on the serpent, and so he had to declare it faithfully; and Deborah saw that the curse would come upon the people who shrank back from suffering for righteousness' sake when God needed them to stand with Him against the foes of His people.

Again, when Moses said that he was putting before Israel "blessing" and "cursing"— blessing if they would obey the law and cursing if they broke it—it was not merely Moses pronouncing it. He was acting as God's representative, declaring what it would be, and the people, knowing this, said, "Amen"—"So be it" or "So let it be." These very words have come to pass to the Jews as a nation, and they have been scattered, riven, hunted, and sent from place to place; for the sole of their feet they have had no rest. Israel also, as a nation, confirmed the curse upon them at Calvary when they said, "His blood be on us, and on our children." They might have been set free from it had they accepted Him who was bearing the curse as the One given by God to bear the sin and the curse of the whole world.

These solemn facts are not clearly seen by many of us, and so we put the emphasis on love and forgiveness. We do not realize that these things are written in the Book by which we shall be judged, and that the only place for love and forgiveness is at Calvary. Judgment, cursing, wrath, and terrible retribution upon sin and Satan must be faced away from the place called Calvary.

Do you remember Elisha and the bears and the young lads, when he "cursed them in the name of the LORD" (2 Kings 2:24)? That was a strange thing! Was it not a lesson of rebuke to those who mocked the men representing God that brought about this terrible dealing—a lesson not to trifle with the God who is at the back of those who speak in His name?

Then we may think of Jeremiah, who said, "Cursed is the man that trusteth in man" (Jeremiah 17:5), and "Blessed is the man . . . whose trust the LORD is" (Jeremiah 17:7). Why not have said, "Poor man, that trusteth in man"? Why say "*Cursed* is the man"? Because in the light of God the working of the law was inevitable: the curse must come on those who trusted in man instead of God, and God's blessing with His richness of life on those who made the Lord their trust. Upon whom, then, do *you* place your trust?

Was Jeremiah pronouncing a curse? No, he was only declaring what his spiritual vision showed him: if man trusted in man, then the curse of God which rested on Satan would come on him because of identification with Satan's own attitude of turning away from God—the very sin into which he beguiled the first Adam.

Again, Jeremiah said, "*Cursed be he that doeth the work of the* LORD *negligently*" (Jeremiah 48:10), that is to say, badly, slovenly, carelessly. It simply means that no work that you can do "for the Lord" will He prosper to make up for laziness! The "curse" must work in connection with it, and a blight come upon it. God's will is done in heaven with alacrity and care. He will not send the Holy Spirit to cooperate with and bless what you do carelessly and without your whole heart. You say that your work is only a trifle, so poor that it is not worth noticing; but there is no "trifle" in God's sight. If you are careless in small things, you will be careless in great. There are many who are asking God's blessing who are too lazy to do His work thoroughly, in a manner that will bring God's blessing. God works no miracle to spare us labor and toil (1 Thessalonians 4:10–12).

It has been said that "holiness and hard work" must succeed, and it is true. Holiness is necessary and must be counted first in importance, but it needs hard work with it. If you want God's blessing, be absolutely faithful in that which is least and do "the small things" as thoroughly as the great ones, for the small things may turn out to be the great ones in the end.

Turning to the Book of Malachi, we read, *"Ye are cursed with the curse; for ye rob Me . . . in tithes and offerings"* (Malachi 3:8–9). Here we find the curse mentioned again (with the emphasized "the" of the Revised Version), this time in connection with the question, "Will a man rob God?" And the lesson again seems to be that there is a law of God operative since the time of the fall in Eden that brings, in sore judgment, the working of the curse upon any wrong attitude to God. Was it *Malachi* pronouncing it? No. As with all the other "prophets" or "representatives" of God, he simply declared what God revealed to him. Religious Israel was "cursed with the curse" because they robbed God by withholding what was due to Him.

Turning to the New Testament for light for

the Gospel dispensation, we have the remarkable passage in Mark 11 where the Lord Jesus
cursed the fig tree, and the disciples said to
Him, "Rabbi, behold, the fig tree which thou
cursedst is withered away" (Mark 11:21). And
the Lord replied, "*Ye shall not only do what is
done to the fig tree,* but even if ye shall say unto
this mountain, Be thou taken up and cast into
the sea, it shall be done" (Matthew 21:21). The
withering of the fig tree was the effect of the
curse.

"YE SHALL NOT ONLY DO WHAT IS DONE TO
THE FIG TREE!" It is remarkable that this inci-
dent is mentioned in connection with some
teaching on prayer: "Have faith in God. Verily I
say unto you, Whosever . . . shall not doubt in
his heart, but shall BELIEVE that WHAT HE SAITH
cometh to pass, he shall have it. Therefore I say
unto you, All things, whatsoever ye pray and
ask for, believe that ye RECEIVE them, and ye
shall have them" (Mark 11:22–24). And "ye
shall not only DO what is done to the fig tree!"
The praying was described as "doing" when it
accomplished mighty things, and the "speak-
ing" was "doing" too. The Lord "cursed" the
fig tree—it withered. Was it that He cooperated
with, or set in motion, so to speak, the law of
the curse working in the world? At least the
truth is clear: the believer is authorized by these
words of the Master to say in prayer, concerning everything that Satan instigates and works

through, "May the curse of God come upon all things that have their *source and inspiration* from the god of this world," whether secular or apparently religious.

When you look out with clear spiritual vision, how much you see of work that will not stand, for it is only built upon the sand. Why not go to God and say, "Oh, Lord, it is just like the fig tree. Let it wither away!" Have you seen any religious "fig trees" with only leaves and no fruit? What have you done when you have seen them? Turned away, and said, "How sad!" Why have you not gone to the Lord and said, "Lord, *wither the 'tree,' so that the workers are not deceived*"? That is the thing to do—not going to others and talking about it, but going to your knees, and asking the Lord to wither what is there that needs to be withered and to strengthen what is of God.

Pray as you go about, "Lord, strengthen what is of God; blight and wither whatever Thou seest should be withered!" But remember, the Lord said, "Ye shall *not only* do what is done to the fig tree"—for that is really a small thing—later on you will see a *"mountain"*! If your faith has reached to the point which withers a fruitless fig tree, *you will then be able to deal with the "mountain,"* and SAY, "BE THOU REMOVED . . . and it shall be done!" "If ye have faith, and doubt not" (Matthew 21:21), if you know that God is at the back of the word, then there will be no doubt in your heart.

Christ did not wither the fig tree out of vindictiveness, nor out of resentment, nor out of revenge; but He did it probably to show His disciples the working of a law. Neither are *you* to pray for the withering power of the curse to come upon "empty leaves" because they are a trial to you. Instead, your prayer must arise from that spiritual purity which comes from union with the reigning Christ, so that you may do the works of Christ.

Further, we have a glimpse of the same deep insight into the working of the curse when we read the declaration of Paul: "If any man preach any other gospel unto you than that which ye received, LET HIM BE ACCURSED!" (Galatians 1:9, KJV). The apostle had clear vision as to what would come to the man who turned aside from the Gospel of Substitution— the truth of Christ bearing our curse for us. If any will not believe that Christ bore the curse for them, then they are bound to remain under the curse and be accursed; for they are under the curse of sin, and identified with the curse on Satan, because they are blinded by him and have been taken captive by him.

What solemn words to speak: "*If any man preach any other gospel unto you than that which ye received,* LET HIM BE ACCURSED!" It is the revelation again of the law of the curse, and of the only hope of escape being at Calvary. If he will not have Christ as the curse for him, then he comes under the curse for himself. In truth, the curse is already upon him, and it is only awaiting the outworking of its blighting results. Think of the man who preaches other than the gospel of the cross of Calvary! It is a blight in itself to blight other people's lives with falsehood, which ends them in a hopeless eternity. It is a blight to have the Christians in other lands turning aside from the atoning work of Jesus Christ because men in England and America preach "another gospel" than the gospel of Calvary. It is an awful thing for preachers and ministers to deepen the curse on men by failure to preach the one divine gospel of the cross of Christ. *"Let him be accursed!"* Let the curse which he refuses to see is upon the Lamb come to its fruition in himself! God's Word has declared it, and it shows us that these things are working today, whether we see them or not.

Now we can understand why the Lord said, *"Depart from Me, ye cursed, into the eternal fire"* (Matthew 25:41). In the description given in Matthew 25 of the judgment of the nations, which shall take place when the Son of Man is come, now we can see beneath the surface of what is written. Their indifference to "the least of these My brethren" was not merely a turning away from the suffering and needy ones; it was a turning away from their Lord, and a turning to and identification with the accursed one—the deceiver of the whole inhabited earth.

There will come an hour when *"There shall be no more curse"* (Revelation 22:3, KJV). Satan will then be in the lake of fire. There will always be the curse among men as long as Satan is among them; mankind cannot get rid of it until they get rid of him. There is nothing said in this Book that warrants the idea that he will be redeemed. Do not delude yourselves with that lie of Satan's. There is no hope given that the curse upon him will end in anything other than the lake of fire, with the false prophet and the beast he has energized. If any of you believe that *Satan will be redeemed,* you are believing a lie that has come to you from deceiving spirits—a lie from the pit. The many doctrines that are abroad today must be brought to the standard of the Word of God.

When your eyes have been opened to see what the devil has done from Eden downwards, and what he is doing in the world today, there will rise from the depths of your spirit—where God dwells—nothing less, nothing else, than an "AMEN" TO THAT CURSE pronounced in Eden upon Satan, and also upon all his hosts of darkness. Those of you who know what the attacks of the powers of darkness are, if you would use a mighty weapon against them, say—as you stand on the ground of Calvary—"One thing is certain, and it is that *you* *are under the curse of God."* Thus you will seize an effective weapon to wield against them. Say, "IT IS WRITTEN . . . CURSED SHALT THOU BE!" Part of the fulfillment of that curse is on the horizon, for the hour is drawing nigh when the prince of darkness, "the old serpent," "he that is called the Devil and Satan," "the deceiver of the whole inhabited earth,"* shall be cast into the pit.

What we need at this time is an infallible weapon for victory. That available weapon, blessed be God, is first to be found in the gospel that you escape from the curse in *Calvary's cross.* As you avail yourself of it you can say to the powers of darkness—who are under the feet of the ascended Lord—"In the name of Jesus, I say 'Amen' to God's curse on you. 'Get you hence.'"

Servants of God, go back to your place of battle and, clothed in the whole armor of God, strengthened with might by the Spirit of God, *use the truth.* Lay hold of the weapons of war prepared for use, and stored in the armory of the Written Word, that "by them thou mayest war the good warfare" (1 Timothy 1:18) and through the Scriptures inspired of God be "furnished completely unto every good work" (2 Timothy 3:17).

Praise God for Calvary! Christ has re-

---

* Revelation 12:9, margin.

deemed us! Yes, *"Christ redeemed us from the curse of the law, having become a curse for us"* (Galatians 3:13).* "Thanks be to God, who giveth us the victory through our Lord Jesus Christ!"

"And they overcame him because of the blood of the Lamb, and because of the word of their testimony; and they loved not their life even unto death" (Revelation 12:11).

---

* "The cross and the curse are inseparable (Deuteronomy 21:22–23; Galatians 3:13). To say our old man has been 'crucified with Him,' 'I have been crucified with Christ' . . . means this: I have seen that my old nature, myself, deserves the curse; that there is no way of getting rid of it but by death: I voluntarily give it to the death . . . I give my old man, my flesh, self, with its will and work, as a sinful accursed thing, to the cross. . . .

"The way in which this faith in the power of the cross, as at once the revelation and the removal of the curse and the power of the flesh works, is very simple. . . . I begin to understand that the one thing I need is: to look upon the 'flesh' as God does: to accept of the death warrant the cross brings . . . to look upon it, and all that comes from it, as an accursed thing. . . ." (*The Spirit of Christ*, by Rev. Dr. Andrew Murray).

Particulars of the magazine
The Overcomer may be obtained from:

The Overcomer Literature Trust
9-11 Clothier Road
Brislington, Bristol BS4 5RL
England.

This book was produced by CLC Publications. We hope it has been helpful to you in living the Christian life. CLC is a literature mission with ministry in over 50 countries worldwide. If you would like to know more about us, or are interested in opportunities to serve with a faith mission, we invite you to write to:

CLC Publications
P.O. Box 1449
Fort Washington, PA 19034